ACT
—with—
Anxiety

An Acceptance and Commitment
Therapy Workbook to Get You Unstuck
from Anxiety and Enrich Your Life

Richard Sears, PsyD, PhD, MBA, ABPP

All identifying information, including names and other details, has been changed to protect the privacy of individuals. This book is not a substitute for continuing education or professional supervision, or for seeking advice from a trained professional. The author and publisher disclaim responsibility for any adverse effects arising from the application of the information contained herein.

Copyright © 2021 by Richard W. Sears
Published by
PESI Publishing & Media
PESI, Inc.
3839 White Ave
Eau Claire, WI 54703

Cover: Amy Rubenzer
Editing: Jenessa Jackson, PhD
Layout: Amy Rubenzer & Bookmasters
ISBN: 9781559570749
All rights reserved.
Printed in the United States of America

PESI
Publishing
& Media
pesipublishing.com

Praise for ACT with Anxiety

"I love this book. It is easy to read and yet never underestimates the reader. It covers the solid core of ACT work, extending over decades, and yet it has a fresh feel with new ways of expressing these ideas. It takes the basic science underneath ACT seriously, and yet it never succumbs to jargon. It is a steady, thorough, practical walk-through of ACT by a person who has devoted many years to mindfulness practice. You can feel the author's balanced presence and authenticity underneath every line. I highly recommend it."

> — Steven C. Hayes, PhD
> Foundation Professor of Psychology, University of Nevada
> Originator and co-developer of Acceptance and Commitment Therapy

"Prepare to learn ACT from a ninja! Richard Sears brings Acceptance and Commitment Therapy to life by discussing Cosmic Self-Meditation, Magic Wands, Superheroes, and much more… but also maintains an intensely practical approach which will help you apply this evidence-based therapeutic approach to your clients' struggle with anxiety. Sears includes great stories and examples, and also provides "Tips for Clinicians" throughout the book in order to truly highlight how an ACT therapist can be maximally effective."

> — D.J. Moran, PhD, BCBA-D
> Institute for Higher Performance

"Master therapist and trainer, Dr. Richard Sears, has written the definitive guide for Acceptance and Commitment Therapy with one of the most common problems experienced by clients and the population at large—anxiety. Few authors write with such clarity, empathy, and most importantly, applicability. From explaining the ins and outs of ACT and anxiety with everyday metaphors and examples to providing easy-to-follow exercises for feeling better, Dr. Sears presents therapists, clients, and laypeople an essential guide to transforming their experience of anxiety. This book is indispensable in these incredibly anxious times."

> — Lane Pederson, PhD
> Author of *The Expanded Dialectical Behavior Therapy Skills Training Manual*

"Richard Sears brings the state of the art of evidence-based practice to the problem of anxiety in this useful, accessible, and brilliant workbook. If you struggle with anxiety, or help people who face this struggle, this book is a must-read addition to your library, and will help you reclaim your life."

> — Dennis Tirch, PhD
> Director, The Center for Compassion Focused Therapy

Dedication

To my daughter Caylee, for her patience with my writing when she wanted to play.

Table of Contents

Chapter 6 — Acceptance: Letting Go of the Battle with Anxious Feelings 119

Chapter 7 — Just This Moment: Breaking Free from Future Worries and Past Regrets 153

Chapter 8 — Just Do It: Taking Committed Action

About the Author

Richard W. Sears, PsyD, PhD, MBA, ABPP, regularly travels across the U.S. giving presentations for PESI. He is a board-certified clinical psychologist in Cincinnati, Ohio, where he runs a private therapy and consultation practice, and is director of the Center for Clinical Mindfulness & Meditation. He has practiced and taught mindfulness for over 35 years, and was full-time faculty for the PsyD Program at Union Institute & University for nine years. He is also an annual adjunct professor of Psychology at the University of Cincinnati, clinical/research faculty at the UC Center for Integrative Health and Wellness, and a volunteer professor of Clinical Psychiatry & Behavioral Neurosciences with the UC College of Medicine. Dr. Sears is also a psychologist contractor with Alliance Integrative Medicine and with the Cincinnati VA Medical Center.

Dr. Sears is author of *The CBT & Mindfulness Toolbox*, *Mindfulness: Living Through Challenges and Enriching Your Life*, *Building Competence in Mindfulness-Based Cognitive Therapy*, *MBCT for PTSD* (with Kathleen Chard), *The Sense of Self*, *Mindfulness in Clinical Practice* (with Dennis Tirch and Robert Denton), *Consultation Skills for Mental Health Professionals* (with John Rudisill and Carrie Mason-Sears), *Hopes and Perspectives of Muslim American Women: A Paradox of Honor* (with Tayeba Shaikh and Jennifer Ossege), and *Group Therapy for Voice Hearers* (with Andrea Lefebvre and Jennifer Ossege). He is co-editor of the books *Perspectives on Spirituality and Religion in Psychotherapy* (with Alison Niblick) and *The Resilient Private Practice* (with Jennifer Ossege).

He is also a fifth-degree black belt in Ninjutsu, and once served as a personal protection agent for the Dalai Lama of Tibet. He has a PhD in Buddhist Studies, and received ordination in three traditions, as well as recognition as a Zen master from Wonji Dharma in the lineage of Seung Sahn.

You can also join an online group or listen to free recordings on Dr. Sears's website, www.psych-insights.com/mindfulness

Acknowledgments

This book is the culmination of years of teaching workshops for mental health professionals on ACT for PESI, Inc. I would like to begin by thanking the many workshop participants who shared their ideas, passions, and questions, challenging me to continuously refine my own understanding. I would also like to thank the wonderful people at PESI and PESI Publishing & Media, including Lauren Hovde, Amy Forsberg, Karsyn Morse, Hillary Jenness, Linda Jackson, Amy Rubenzer, Jenessa Jackson, Kate Sample, Anna Rustick, Nicole Rate, Kay Friske, Emily Krumenauer, Shannon Todd, Josh Lindblad, Claire Zelasko, and Shannon Becker.

Many thanks to Jan Karuna Bodhi Grafton for her painstaking work in transcribing the entire ACT workshop that I did in Charleston, WV, which this book is based upon. I also appreciate the beautiful drawings she contributed to this book.

As with everything in life, the content of this workbook is the product of a great many influences. I have been trained and inspired by so many others that it is quite possible (and in fact highly likely) that I used many of their ideas without acknowledging them, but I will do my best to give credit where it is due.

I would especially like to thank the many ACT pioneers and trainers who have created and shared a life-changing approach to therapy, and who always so kindly and so freely give their knowledge and their time: Steven C. Hayes, Kelly Wilson, Kirk Strosahl, D.J. Moran, Kevin Polk, Dennis Tirch, Robyn Walser, John and Jamie Forsyth, Hank Robb, Russ Harris, JoAnne Dahl, Jason Luoma, Niklas Torneke, and countless others.

I am also very appreciative of the support and inspiration of countless professional colleagues, friends, and mentors on the path of self-exploration, including the Dalai Lama, Wonji Dharma, Suhita Dharma, Stephen K. Hayes, Zindel Segal, Jon Kabat-Zinn, Elana Rosenbaum, Lane Pederson, Marsha Linehan, Susan Woods, Randye Semple, Jean Kristeller, Ryan Niemiec, Susan Albers, Sarah Bowen, Ruth Baer, Mark Lau, Alan Marlatt, Dan Siegel, Alan Watts, Sian Cotton, Melissa DelBello, Jeffery Strawn, Rachel Wasson, Kathleen Chard, Tina Luberto, Kristen Kraemer, Emily O'Bryan, Jennifer Ossege, Steve and Sandi Amoils, Robert Brian Denton, Sharon Salzberg, David Kyutoshi Sink, David Piser, and John Ryongwan Paulson, to name but a few.

And of course, I am very thankful for the love and support of my family, and for their patience with my countless days of isolation to write and to travel to give workshops: Carrie Mason-Sears, Ashlyn & Lizon Karim, Caylee Sears, Olivia and Brittney and Violet Taylor, and Linda and John Coghill. I also appreciate the wonderful drawings my daughters contributed to this book.

Finally, I would like to thank my students and clients for sharing so much of their suffering and their joys with me. While I have changed details to protect their identities, their stories greatly enrich the material in this workbook. I feel honored and privileged to have shared such profound human journeys with them.

Introduction

Anxiety, in all its various forms, is one of the most common mental health challenges today. Ironically, the more intensely one tries to avoid or control it, the worse it tends to get. Worrying sparks anxiety, and anxiety sparks more worrying. People with anxiety develop a pattern in which they avoid doing things and going places to try to get away from the feelings of anxiety, which makes their lives increasingly more restricted, which ironically perpetuates the anxiety. People can literally go their entire lives stuck in this cycle.

Because we do not like to see our clients suffer, well-intentioned therapists can inadvertently make clients worse by trying to teach them to avoid their unpleasant thoughts and feelings. While this sometimes works temporarily, especially for mild cases of anxiety, it tends to backfire with more serious cases, and can accidentally feed a longer-term struggle. Both client and therapist can become caught in the same cycle of avoidance and frustration.

Older forms of psychotherapy taught clients with anxiety to challenge the validity and rationality of their anxious thoughts, but newer research shows that this often intensifies the struggle, especially if done confrontationally, thereby increasing the anxiety. Challenging thoughts can inadvertently give them more power. **A deeper understanding of how thoughts are conditioned by experience and emotion has allowed new breakthroughs in working with the most difficult anxiety disorders.**

Because anxiety is unpleasant by definition, it takes courage and motivation to face it. For many people, their anxiety becomes so intense, and so overwhelming, that they get stuck in a survival mode, and life becomes drudgery. Their very identities can become overly enmeshed with their struggles, and they can get lost in storms of distressing thoughts and feelings.

Tip for Clinicians

Throughout this workbook, important considerations will be highlighted in these "Tips for Clinicians" boxes. The first important tip is to learn to be accepting of your own anxiety if you are going to work with clients with anxiety. If you give off a sense that anxiety cannot be tolerated, and you compulsively try to make them feel better, you might be teaching them avoidance.

Acceptance and Commitment Therapy was pioneered and developed by Steven C. Hayes and colleagues (Hayes, Strosahl, & Wilson, 2012). The abbreviation, ACT, is pronounced as one word to emphasis the action component of this approach. (If you pronounce each letter separately, people will immediately know you have only read about ACT.)

More of an empirically grounded process approach than another rigid school of psychotherapy, ACT can incorporate any evidence-based intervention. ACT uses acceptance and mindfulness processes to help people relate differently to distressing thoughts and feelings and also utilizes commitment and behavioral change processes to help them flexibly move in the direction of a more fulfilling life (Hayes, Strosahl, Bunting, Twohig, & Wilson, 2004).

ACT is an evidence-based intervention with decades of research support. Before sharing it with the public, Dr. Hayes and his colleagues spent years looking into the foundational principles, doing controlled research, and refining the concepts and techniques. While many therapies start with someone creating a system and hoping that later research supports it, the ACT developers started from the ground up. They looked at the big picture of what actually works in therapy. They built on principles like classical conditioning, negative reinforcement, and exposure therapy. They looked at the techniques and concepts that were consistently clinically effective in the research and discovered the principles that fit them together. Therefore, ACT does not discount any evidence-based treatment technique, as we will discuss in the next chapter on ACT processes.

Interestingly, I went to a conference years ago for the Association for Behavioral and Cognitive Therapies. A panel of big names in psychotherapy was assembled to have a case discussion about how they would treat an individual struggling with a substance use disorder. The panel consisted of Arthur Freeman, an expert on cognitive therapy; Howard Kassinove, an expert on anger management; Raymond "Chip" Tafrate, an expert on motivational interviewing and forensic cognitive behavioral therapy (CBT); and Steven C. Hayes. During their conversations, and in response to questions from audience members, these experts would literally say things like, "Oh you know, I think I would rather have Steve deal with this kind of thing." And Dr. Hayes would say, "Hmmm, motivational interviewing might be a good thing to do in that situation, what do you think, Chip?" It's so funny to me how sometimes the "disciples" of certain therapeutic orientations are more rigid about it than the creators are. Leaders in the field are often just creative people trying to help others with their suffering and are not trying to create a limited belief system. It is important for clinical experience and research to be guides for homing in on what really works and not to just do something because some so-called "expert" says it should be effective.

ACT is an evidence-based treatment for a wide variety of presenting issues. A few years ago, the number of ACT research subjects in randomized controlled trials (RCTs) surpassed 10,000! There have been over 300 RCTs using ACT, several dozen of which were specific to anxiety (ACBS, 2020). You will find ACT RCTs have been done in countries around the globe, including England, Ireland, Iran, China, Sweden, Australia, Korea, India, Cyprus, and others. The number of studies is growing constantly, because the ACT community has a plethora of robust and collaborative researchers.

ACT is considered a "third wave" approach that builds on the foundations of CBT. Behavioral therapy was the first wave, and cognitive therapy was the second wave. ACT expands upon the research foundations developed in the first two waves. ACT shares some common ground with other third wave approaches like mindfulness-based cognitive therapy (MBCT; Segal, Williams, & Teasdale, 2013) and dialectical behavior therapy (DBT; Linehan, 1993, 2014). The various third wave practitioners consider each other "fellow travelers on the path."

DBT was primarily designed for individuals with borderline personality disorder, and is a wonderful, in-depth program for learning a wide variety of skills for improving one's life. MBCT is designed to be an eight-week program for developing a deep understanding of mindfulness and how thoughts and emotions work, and is primarily designed to prevent problems from coming back in the future. From the very beginning, ACT has been designed to be a "full-service" therapy. It can incorporate principles from MBCT, DBT, and every other evidence-based treatment. ACT can be used in individual therapy, couples therapy, and group therapy. It has also been applied in areas outside of therapy, like teaching, coaching, and organizational consultation.

In this workbook, the principles and concepts of using ACT with anxiety will be elaborated upon through clinical case examples and stories. Through both "big picture" principles and specific, practical, clinical techniques, you will be equipped with new perspectives and tools that you can immediately integrate into your clinical practice, whatever your theoretical orientation. The worksheets will give you opportunities to process your own experiences with the concepts and exercises. In addition, you can give handouts to your clients to help them understand and deal better with generalized anxiety, panic, health anxiety, obsessive-compulsive disorders, trauma, and other types of anxiety-related issues.

Many therapists get frustrated when they know how to help clients with anxiety, but those clients are not willing to do the work. When we can help clients find or rediscover their big-picture life values, they become more motivated. This workbook will also help clients get in touch with their values, and help them incorporate the scientific principles of ACT into their daily moments between therapy sessions.

Research shows that if you do the things in life that matter to you, your suffering is likely to go down (Gloster et al., 2017). However, if you first try to get rid of your suffering, you will not necessarily end up living a meaningful life. When we can find an important reason to live, we are more willing to allow even unpleasant thoughts, distressing emotions, and physical discomfort to be present when they show up. No one wants to deal with problems or feel uncomfortable, but if we can identify and move toward what really matters, our lives become richer and more meaningful.

Tip for Clinicians

Note that this book is called ACT with Anxiety, not get rid of anxiety first then act. Watch out for a focus on getting rid of the anxiety—the goal is to help the client create a life worth living, even if there is some anxiety that comes along for the ride.

While this workbook will focus on practical principles and techniques that you may be able to apply right away, if you are going to use this with clients, it is crucially important to get experiential training in ACT. Now don't worry, as an introvert myself, I'm happy to report that you don't have to do things like stand up on a table and cluck like a chicken. However, just reading and talking about ACT is not enough. Words are just one aspect of the human experience. When everything is filtered through words, sometimes we can get stuck in those words, or stuck in the client's words. I'm not necessarily talking about something mystical here—it is simply that the words of the thinking mind are very limited, and life is so much richer and more complex than words can describe.

Because ACT is much more than working with thoughts, do not be concerned if you feel like you just do not "get it" intellectually. **The things we can think about and explain in a linear fashion with words are only a small representation of reality.** ACT utilizes a number of non-verbal processes, and experience and practice will give you an increasingly deeper sense of this approach over time. In fact, even the people who are ACT authors and experts will often say, "You know, I do ACT, and I even teach ACT, but I'm not really sure I totally get it."

In fact, an interesting study illustrates this point (Lappalainen, Lehtonen, Skarp, Taubert, Ojanen, & Hayes, 2007). A group of graduate students working in a university counseling center were randomized into two different groups. One group was taught to use CBT with their clients. The other group was trained in ACT. After the trainings, they were told to use only that particular approach with their clients for a period of time. Afterward, the researchers interviewed the therapists to ask them how it went. Those trained in CBT basically said, "Oh, I feel pretty good about how things went. I felt like I knew what I was doing. I understood the principles and was able to structure the sessions." The ACT students basically said, "I'm not sure I fully knew what to do, but I followed the principles as best I could. I'm not really sure how it went." And you know what? In this particular study, the clients of the ACT therapists had better symptom improvement.

What strikes me about this study is that **sometimes we do what is most comfortable for us, which may not necessarily be what is best for the client.** The ACT approach is about meeting clients where they are, acknowledging the reality of their suffering, and taking steps alongside them in their journey toward a more fulfilling life.

I was honored to receive an appreciative email once from a client who had been struggling with her challenges for many years, which can be common for ACT therapists. The email basically said, "Thank you for just staying with me, no matter what was going on. I've had a lot of other therapists, and whenever I wasn't doing well, I often felt a sense of blame from the therapist. I was made to feel as if my not getting better was my own fault, like I wasn't trying hard enough, or I wasn't doing things right." My attitude is, "Well if it's not working, we're both missing something, so let's see where we are and where you want to go." That attitude is very important in therapy. Successful ACT work involves a willingness for us to be in that uncertainty and not to compulsively run away from it or to automatically try to pin it down with words.

Unless you were lucky enough to be born with a gift to do this work, most of us have struggled with that experience of uncertainty, especially when we were brand-new therapists. Do you remember what it was like to be a psychotherapy student? Many of us approached clients with pre-conceived notions. "All right, I think I saw on the intake report that they have obsessive-compulsive disorder (OCD), so I'm going to brush up on all the information I can find about OCD. I'm going to develop a plan, and I'll know exactly what I'm going to do." Then the client walks in the door, and within five minutes, you realize, "Oh no! This person doesn't have OCD. They must have read that on the internet or something. Now what am I going to do?!" You became stuck, because you tried to figure it all out with just your thinking.

While preparation, especially early on in your career, can be very important, you eventually learn to just meet the client in the moment. You learn to trust the process. You stay present as things unfold. You do much better work that way. In fact, my favorite sessions happen when clients walk in the door and say, "I don't have anything to talk about today, but I figured I shouldn't cancel my appointment, so here I am." Those are often some of the best sessions, because by not getting distracted with preconceived plans, we can be open to really exploring completely new experiences and insights.

Tip for Clinicians

Get involved! If you only read about ACT, you might end up just fueling more thinking and struggle with yourself and your clients. ACT is not just something you do to your clients. It is an experiential approach, and it is important for you to experience it for yourself.

If you are sincere about using ACT, I highly recommend joining the Association for Contextual Behavioral Sciences (ACBS) at https://contextualscience.org. ACBS is an insightful and supportive community of ACT practitioners and researchers, and members have access to a wide range of resources, including listservs, ACT videos, online lessons, and client handouts. To gain in-person experiential trainings, I highly recommend attending an ACT Boot Camp, through the ACBS training organization called Praxis, at https://www.praxiscet.com/.

Additionally, for a wealth of live trainings, videos, online courses, and resources on ACT, mindfulness, and other important topics, visit www.pesi.com.

I also invite you to connect with me. Visit my website, www.psych-insights.com to sign up for an eight-week online mindfulness program, and to access free mindfulness recordings you can download and practice on your own. Sign up for my email list to receive tips on ACT and mindfulness, and information about programs and retreats.

In case you were wondering how I got involved with ACT, it probably goes back to when I was a teenager, and I wanted to be a ninja. The funny thing is that Stephen K. Hayes (not to be confused with ACT founder Steven C. Hayes), the person who moved to Japan in 1975 and found the last living ninja grandmaster, lives in Dayton, Ohio of all places, not far from my home. I've been training with him for over 35 years.

Of course, real ninja training is not at all like what you see in the movies. Our lineage can be traced back for 34 generations, over 800 years. When you hear about the ninja being invisible, what that actually means is you don't make a target of yourself. Whenever possible, you work to set up your life in such a way that conflict does not arise in the first place. When you want to make changes in the world, you set up the causes and conditions for those changes to happen. Making a big show of force tends to generate resistance in others. Obviously, doing those things involves developing the mind, which led me to delve into the practices of mindfulness and meditation.

When I became a young adult, I opened my own martial arts school, and I also taught meditation classes. Perhaps because they viewed me as a teacher, my students began telling me about their life problems, relationship issues, and mental health challenges. This eventually led me to getting my doctorate degree in clinical psychology. I received in-depth generalist training, and I got to do almost everything in a psychologist's scope of practice (under supervision of course). After I finished my post-doc and got licensed, I became full-time core faculty in a doctor of clinical psychology program. This forced me to keep up with the latest research and the different evidence-based clinical interventions. ACT was just starting to become popular then, and it fit very well with my research interests and with my personal experiences. I've been involved with quite a few mindfulness studies, such as using MBCT with veterans with PTSD (posttraumatic stress disorder), using an abbreviated MBCT program for providers, and teaching mindfulness to the general public. I was also privileged to be the clinical lead in the first mindfulness study that used brain scans for kids and adolescents.

Although I still maintain a number of academic and research affiliations, I've always had a private psychotherapy practice, which is now my main professional focus, along with writing and teaching workshops. My real passion is to make interventions like ACT usable and concrete. The research literature on ACT can at times seem quite dense and recondite, given that these concepts can be challenging to operationalize in words. While I encourage you to dive into the research to understand ACT more thoroughly, this workbook will focus on the essential principles and the practical applications. Since ACT can incorporate every other evidence-based treatment, keep doing whatever you are already doing right now that works. By adding some broader concepts, principles, and skills, my hope is that you will help even more individuals become increasingly free from their struggles and lead richer, more fulfilling lives.

I invite you to enter into a realm of science beyond words, and to explore a deeper sense of fulfillment in uncertainty.

Are you willing to jump in?

Tip for Clinicians ────────────────────────────────────

As you read through this workbook, do all of the worksheets yourself. We are human beings just like our clients, and it is important to understand and digest these concepts and processes. It will make you a better, more empathic clinician, and as an added bonus, it may just enrich your own life.

Chapter

1

The Anxiety Trap and How to ACT

In this chapter, we will explore how people get caught in anxiety traps, and how avoidance perpetuates and exacerbates it. This chapter will also provide an overview of ACT and its underlying principles and processes.

Anxiety is very common in both clinical settings and in the general population. It runs on a continuum from mild and situational to severe and pervasive.

Tip for Clinicians ————————————————————————

Clients often already feel bad that they have worked so hard but cannot get rid of their anxiety. Emphasize that this is not their fault—it is how the human brain works—and they are doing what they think will help the anxiety go down in the short run. They just need to learn a different strategy for long-term living.

ANXIETY AND THE PROBLEM OF AVOIDANCE

Clients (and therapists too) can often forget that anxiety is a normal, and in fact important, part of daily life. Anxiety is the stress response firing up to tell us to pay attention. The goal is not to get rid of anxiety, but to understand its function.

For example, if you have an important test to take (like a licensure exam), you are likely to feel anxiety. If you have no anxiety at all about the test, you will not feel motivated to study for it, and you will not focus on doing well while you are taking it. Of course, if the anxiety is very high, and you begin to battle with the anxiety, you will also not be able to focus very well on the test.

Anxiety is not an enemy, it is a natural function of the human body. However, through the process of negative reinforcement, it can be perpetuated. As we know, if you avoid a situation that causes anxiety, the anxiety lowers, reinforcing the avoidance behavior. When you have anxiety, you don't want to feel it. No rational human being wants to be anxious, but that avoidance can come with a cost, the cost of not fully participating in meaningful activities.

Now, at a more subtle level, thinking itself can be a distraction, and therefore a form of avoidance, so **worrying and ruminating can be negatively reinforced**. When you are anxious, your attention is often on your thinking, and you don't notice your body as much in that moment. While you're giving your attention to your thinking, it seems like your anxiety is decreasing when in actuality, you're just distracted. Your brain basically says, "Whatever you're doing right now, the anxiety is not as intense as when I'm tuned into my body, so do more of whatever it is you're doing (which in this case is thinking)." This is why people can be up all night ruminating and worrying, and why they can't stop thinking about something all throughout the day. If they stop thinking, they feel their body sensations more, and the anxiety is felt more acutely. This process, known as the extinction burst, occurs because now they are feeling it directly and not distracting themselves with thoughts. Though not consciously, they tell themselves that feeling is a terrible idea, so they go back into their heads. To make things even worse, the thoughts often trigger more anxiety, but they don't want to feel the anxiety in the body, so they go back in their heads, which triggers more anxiety.

This is why people can go their whole lives with anxiety. In order to break out of this cycle, clients (and perhaps some therapists) will need to do something completely different.

The following handouts are meant to normalize clients' experiences of having anxiety or trauma-related symptoms. Once they feel understood, they are more likely to be willing to engage in the work of therapy. Also included is a handout for insomnia, since this is a common issue for people with anxiety.

Anxiety and the Avoidance Trap

Maybe you've had anxiety as long as you can remember, or maybe it came on fairly recently. Maybe your genes made you more prone to it, or maybe the people around you taught you to be more sensitive to it. Or maybe you've just been dealt more than your fair share of difficult troubles in your life.

It may have started off as such a little thing. Nobody likes to feel anxious, so you started avoiding situations that were likely to cause it. Driving a car, especially in busy traffic, creates anxiety, so maybe you began deciding more and more often that it's just easier to stay home. Maybe you get a little nervous being around strangers, so it felt safer to just spend more and more of your time alone. Maybe you can force yourself to do things, but you practically hold your breath the whole time to endure the anxiety until you can get away from it again. Ironically, even though you are trying your best not to feel those uncomfortable feelings of anxiety, they just seem to keep coming back. There may be periods when it seems better, but you may be finding that it is getting worse over time.

Anxiety can manifest itself in a number of ways. Maybe you can't stop thinking about certain things. Maybe you find yourself doing certain behaviors as a way to control the anxiety, even though you know logically that they don't work very well. Maybe you can't stop worrying about your health. Maybe your anxiety sometimes gets so strong that it leads to panic attacks.

How did things get this bad? What went wrong? How did anxiety come to rule your life? Why can't you just use willpower to get past this?

Well, **you may have accidentally fallen into the anxiety trap**.

For what it's worth, intelligent people are more likely to suffer from anxiety, so that tells me that at least you're smart. Unfortunately, your brain can sometimes work against itself. The things that are usually good for solving problems in the external world can actually prolong anxiety.

Believe it or not, your brain is actually trying to help you with its ideas and spiraling thoughts. It wants you to avoid the anxiety, because it doesn't feel good. The smarter you are, the more clever you can be about how to avoid anxiety.

While avoidance is sometimes helpful in the short run, it's a terrible long-term strategy. You can avoid situations that make you anxious, but then your life becomes smaller and less fulfilling. Even thinking can be a distraction from the uncomfortable feelings, as your brain tries to help by worrying and ruminating so that you are in your head rather than in your body.

You may have even turned to alcohol, or a certain type of medication called benzodiazepines. While they may help you feel better in the moment, they don't really address the bigger issues. Also, while some people experience very few withdrawal symptoms, others have a very tough time getting off of these types of medications. There is also a phenomenon known as **the rebound effect**. Basically, your brain wants to settle into a balanced state. So, when a medication puts more of a certain chemical into your brain, you make less of it, or your receptors for that chemical begin to die off. If you stop taking the medication, your brain will actually be worse than it was before, and it will take some time for your brain to regrow the receptors it had.

Of course, sometimes medications are very helpful. Talk to a medical professional about your specific circumstances. My point is simply to be careful when you expect the medication to fix everything, and to watch for the times when the meds might be making things worse.

Whether through medication, thinking, or running away, most people just want to avoid their anxiety, and these things can be helpful in the short run. **It seems so backwards that avoidance makes things worse in the long run!** After all, wouldn't any human being want to avoid anxiety?

The good news is that we know why people like you get caught in these traps, and there are effective ways out. You don't have to stay like this forever.

Have you ever seen a Chinese finger trap? It's a classic child's toy, but it can teach us an important lesson. Once your fingers are inside, the harder you try to pull your fingers out, the tighter the trap becomes. You can work really hard for hours, doing the logical thing of trying to pull your fingers out, only to wear yourself out completely. Ironically, the only way out of the trap is to push your fingers into it.

It makes no logical sense, but **the research shows that with anxiety, the only way out of the trap is to move into it in a special way.** Your brain will tell you that you just need to try harder, but since that hasn't been working, you cannot rely on what seems logical.

There could be a lot of different factors contributing to your anxiety, such as thyroid levels or medication side effects, so be sure you are working closely with a medical and mental health professional who can create a treatment plan for your specific needs.

The Trauma Trap

One moment everything seems okay, the next moment you are scared, with your heart racing.

You tell yourself everything is fine, but the feelings won't go away. Your entire body feels like it is on high alert, even though you know there is no threat.

It is an old feeling, and you are tired of it. It has cost you so much—missed experiences, lost relationships, the ability to feel safe in your own skin, the peacefulness of quiet moments.

And to top it all, it is not your fault that all these problems are affecting you. You experienced a horrible trauma, maybe even at the hands of someone who did it on purpose.

You are not crazy. Your brain is doing what it is designed to do. But most likely, no one taught you how this process works, so you are doing what seems logical. Unfortunately, what seems logical is keeping you in this trap.

Because what you experienced was so terrible, you don't want to remember the events or the feelings you had. Many people who experience trauma have trouble believing it really happened, maybe in part because other people deny it or think you are exaggerating. Or maybe you were threatened not to tell.

So, you learned how to avoid, and you might sometimes be really good at it. But it is hard to keep that up all the time, especially as you grow older, and maybe the old thoughts, images, and feelings have been intruding more and more into your life.

Something once happened to me that illustrates how this vicious cycle can happen. I regularly fly all over the U.S. to give workshops, and one day, there were thunderstorms spread out all over the middle part of the country. I flew out of my hometown of Cincinnati, had a layover in Chicago, and needed to get to Kansas to give a presentation. Because of the weather, my flight out of Cincinnati was delayed, and when we got to Chicago, we had to circle in a holding pattern for a while before we could land, waiting for a clearing in the weather.

By the time we landed, I barely made it to the gate for my connecting flight, but it had been canceled because of the storms. Since the show must go on, I eventually found someone who could set me up with another option—flying down to Texas, then back up to Kansas, hoping I could get around the weather. I got on the flight to Texas just before they closed the boarding door, and sat down in a window seat over the wing. Shortly after takeoff, the plane entered the clouds. Right in front of my eyes, a lightning bolt hit the wing! Everyone jumped and gasped at the loud crackling sound, and I was a bit blinded by the light. Intellectually, I know planes are designed to safely discharge the energy without hurting the plane, but that image was literally burned into my mind. I watched lightning off in the distance for the rest of that flight.

By the time we landed in Texas, it was getting late, so the plane to Kansas took off in the dark. We got up to our cruising altitude about six miles up, and were enjoying our complimentary beverages, when suddenly a loud bang shook the entire plane. It felt like a giant hit the plane with a massive hammer, or like we ran over giant speed bumps in the sky. After it happened a second time, we all apologized for spilling our drinks on our neighbors.

Then, it felt like the plane took a hard nosedive. I remember watching ice cubes rolling around on the ceiling as my stomach felt like it was flying out of my mouth. I had a thought that we might all die in a plane crash, as the drop went on for what felt like a long time, though it was probably only about 20 or 30 seconds. As the plane leveled off, the ice cubes all fell to the floor, and we all breathed a sigh of relief. We had only hit a quickly dropping pocket of air, and the plane was fine, but we were all glad to get back on the ground after that.

By the time I got to the hotel, it was almost 2 a.m., and I had to give a presentation early the next morning. As I lay on the bed with my eyes closed, guess what I experienced? Flashes of lightning in my mind, and feelings of being startled in my body. I still strongly felt that sense of my stomach coming out of my mouth and the feelings of fear I had when the plane was dropping.

Luckily, I know how trauma works, so **I just observed the thoughts and images without trying to stop them, and let my feelings come and go without trying to control them**. It was not at all pleasant or fun, but I eventually drifted off to sleep.

It is normal to have strong feelings and to have things flash through your mind for a while after you experience something scary. However, not everyone goes on to develop PTSD, in which the symptoms continue for long periods of time after the trauma has occurred.

Had I tried to distract myself from the thoughts with television, or had I drank alcohol to get rid of the unpleasant feelings, I could have set myself up for a pattern of internal avoidance. Had I refused to get on another airplane after that, I could have set myself up for a pattern of external avoidance. While a little avoidance and distraction are not always bad, **consistently avoiding situations, thoughts, and feelings is what fuels the cycle of PTSD.**

My experience was probably nothing compared to what you went through, so of course you may find it very challenging not to get caught up in the cycle of struggling with PTSD. Don't blame yourself. Those feelings and memories can be very unpleasant, if not downright terrifying.

Now that you have a better understanding of PTSD, one of the hardest things to do will be to let go of doing what has not been working. Avoidance does work in the short run, so you might think you can just keep doing it, but what has it cost you in the long run? What have you had to give up in your life?

The good news is that we now have a much better understanding of PTSD, and we have effective treatments for it. However, even if all this makes sense to you logically, it can be very challenging to work through it by yourself. Be sure to find a competent therapist to help you work through your anxiety and to help guide you toward a richer, more fulfilling life. Of course, you should also consult with a competent medical doctor to rule out any biological factors that might be contributing to what you're experiencing.

What to Do When You Can't Sleep

If you suffer from anxiety, I'll bet you've had many sleepless nights. After all, anxiety is your body's amped up stress response. Your stress system was designed to keep you awake to be alert for danger. When the feeling of danger is sparked, you start thinking about how to manage it, and your body gets ready for action. Unfortunately, when you aren't getting enough sleep, everything is more difficult to deal with, and your stress goes up even more, creating a vicious cycle.

There can be many causes of insomnia, but first of all, make sure you're not doing things that might be making things worse. Drinking alcohol can relax your muscles and help you fall asleep, but it interferes with your body's ability to get into the deeper stages of sleep.

Caffeine is another trap. To help you wake up, you might want a lot of coffee or other stimulant drinks. If you drink a lot of caffeine throughout the day to help you focus, the caffeine can also make you feel more anxious, and can make it harder to sleep the next night. Try to limit the amount of caffeine you have each day, and it is best not to drink it in the afternoon. The "half-life" of caffeine is about six hours—so if you have two cups of coffee in the afternoon, it will be like you just drank one cup of coffee at bedtime.

Try to limit screen time (TV, computer, phones, tablets) before bed—the light activates a part of your brain that thinks it is daytime and may stimulate you to stay awake.

Lower the room temperature. Interestingly, the temperature of the room may be more important than the time you go to bed. Since it gets cooler at night, the brain thinks it must be sleeping time when your room is cool.

Taking long naps during the day may seem like a good idea when you are tired, but can confuse your body, and make it harder to fall asleep at night. If you must take a nap, set an alarm for 15-20 minutes.

If you notice your thoughts racing when you lay down to sleep, pay attention to your breathing. Taking deep breaths activates the relaxation response and gives your mind something to focus on besides worrying. When you get lost in your thoughts, it's like watching a good movie. You get pulled into the emotions and the drama. Step back and just let the movie play—you don't have to get lost in it or try to stop it. If I were to say, "Mary had a little…" your mind would probably say "lamb" automatically. If your mind says, "It's time to go to bed," you will probably automatically think, "I'm not going to sleep." It's just what the mind has been programmed to do, so just relate to those thoughts like a dog yapping at you. It's annoying, but arguing will only make things worse.

Okay, now for **the most important and the most challenging task**: When you can't sleep, **do nothing**. Because ironically, everything you do to try to fall asleep is interfering with a natural process. Sleep can only happen by itself. You can't *make* yourself fall asleep.

If nothing else, consider just lying there as resting your body.

You might also find this story interesting. There once was a woman who said she had not slept in 20 years. An astonishing claim! Scientists were very eager to study this woman, because we thought human beings could not live without regular sleep. However, when they put her in a sleep lab, it turned out that she slept at least 6 hours a night! She kept opening her eyes, and saying, "see, I'm not sleeping," then falling back asleep.

It's entirely possible that you are sleeping more than you think you are. The brain operates on cycles of sleepiness and alertness, and you may not be aware of or remember those transitions.

Of course, there can also be medical reasons that you are having trouble sleeping, like apnea or restless leg syndrome, so it may be important to see a medical doctor or sleep specialist if your insomnia continues.

DEFINING ACCEPTANCE AND COMMITMENT THERAPY

Let's start with a long definition of ACT to give you an overall sense of what this approach is all about.

A Long Definition of ACT

ACT is a functional contextual therapy approach based on Relational Frame Theory which views human psychological problems dominantly as problems of psychological inflexibility fostered by cognitive fusion and experiential avoidance. In the context of a therapeutic relationship, ACT brings direct contingencies and indirect verbal processes to bear on the experiential establishment of greater psychological flexibility primarily through acceptance, defusion, establishment of a transcendent sense of self, contact with the present moment, values, and building larger and larger patterns of committed action linked to those values.

—Steven C. Hayes, contextualscience.org

The above definition of ACT appears rather complicated, but it will be useful to examine. If ACT is brand new to you, you might get confused as we go through this definition, but allowing yourself to feel confused might not be a bad thing. If you think you understand all this only in words, you're going to limit yourself. Learning ACT is not necessarily like learning an academic subject, where you are always building on what you learned before. Learning ACT involves a kind of ongoing, deepening refinement, and maybe even some unlearning of what we thought we knew. So just bear with me as best you can as we walk through this definition to get the big picture. We will then go into more detail throughout the rest of this workbook.

ACT is a functional contextual...

Functional contextualism in a foundational scientific principle in ACT. It basically emphasizes that any behavior needs to be examined in the context of when and where it is happening, and that the function of that behavior needs to be considered. For example, take the behavior of walking. If you only describe my physical body as legs swinging back and forth, that's not walking. You have to recognize there is a floor, and that there is space around me. I am only walking in relationship to the environment against which my speed can be measured (context). Also, what is the function of that behavior? Am I going somewhere, or am I exercising on a treadmill?

Anxiety and avoidance are not always bad in certain contexts and when it serves a certain function. If I am walking down a deserted street and a stranger approaches me while yelling (context), my anxiety will activate my fight-or-flight response to save my life, and I run away from that situation (function). However, if I get anxiety in a jovial social engagement, I may choose to fight that anxiety, and run away from people that I care about.

...therapy approach...

Instead of being merely a collection of techniques, ACT is an approach to therapy, and hence there is great flexibility in how it can be used with clients. Basically, any evidence-based treatment that helps clients move toward a more fulfilling life can be used in the committed action stage, as we will discuss later.

For example, we know that exposure therapy is one of the best ways to treat anxiety, but it can be very uncomfortable. Nobody wants to be uncomfortable. However, the ACT processes can help clients let go of their struggles with their thoughts and feelings, and can help them get in touch with a bigger reason to engage with the exposure techniques (such as spending more time with family).

...based on Relational Frame Theory...

Relational Frame Theory (RFT) has to do with how words and language get conditioned with meanings, associations, and emotions (Torneke, Barnes-Holmes, & Hayes, 2010). While these conditionings can be very useful, when we forget that our own minds give words emotion and power, we can get into some serious trouble.

...which views human psychological problems dominantly as problems of psychological inflexibility...

ACT views psychological inflexibility as a major factor in clients' struggles. Decades ago, Steven Hayes and his colleagues carefully looked through the Diagnostic and Statistical Manual of Mental Disorders (DSM®) in search of a common theme across disorders. They realized that inflexibility was an important factor in all of them, at least to some degree. Clients struggle when they lose their flexibility in dealing with things. They try to control their emotions and thoughts, or they relate to people or situations in a rigid manner. They are trying to do the same thing over and over again, and they expect a different result, or they don't persist when it would be helpful to persist.

...fostered by cognitive fusion and experiential avoidance...

This inflexibility is maintained by cognitive fusion and experiential avoidance. Cognitive fusion refers to the tendency to get stuck in thoughts as if they are real things. It can feel as if you are fused to or stuck inside the thought. When someone has the thought "I am a terrible person," it feels as if that is who they are. The thought seems to have a lot of "stickiness" to it. It has become fused with emotions, meanings, and memories. ACT teaches a process called defusion, which is the ability to recognize "Oh, I'm having a *thought* that I am a terrible person. That's not who I am. I am simply having that thought." This process helps us to get some perspective on our thinking. It is hard to be flexible when you are stuck in your thoughts.

Experiential avoidance also keeps you inflexible. If I'm afraid of my own emotions, and I don't want to feel them, I will try to avoid them, or I will try to avoid situations that might spark those feelings. In my attempts to avoid uncomfortable feelings, I will even avoid important things and activities like work and family. My behavior will become more and more restricted, and I will not be able to deal with situations flexibly.

In the context of a therapeutic relationship...

All therapists know that a good therapeutic relationship is very important. Meta-analyses of psychotherapy show that around 30 percent of change in psychotherapy is accounted for simply by having a good relationship with the client (Wampold & Imel, 2015). However, when I share this research with students, inevitably, they ask, "Well, how do you have a good relationship with clients?" You may have your own answers, depending on your theoretical orientation, but most schools of therapy only hint at this in a vague manner. Interestingly, when research on the therapeutic relationship was conducted with the six ACT processes (which we will discuss soon), the relationship factors washed out (Hayes, 2004, 2008). In other words, if you are doing the six processes of ACT (you are present with them in the moment, you see them as more than their problems, you are defused from their thinking, you are accepting of the emotions they have, and you are committed to moving them toward their values), you will have a good therapeutic relationship.

...ACT brings direct contingencies and indirect verbal processes to bear...

ACT has a behavioral therapy foundation, so it brings direct contingencies into the therapeutic sessions. Therapists take action and involve the client in behavioral experiments, not just conversations.

Because human beings are talkers, ACT also uses indirect verbal processes. Even though fusion with words and thinking can create a lot of problems, we are going to leverage language to our advantage to help our clients. In ACT, we use a lot of metaphors and analogies. Using words to paint pictures, we can start to shift our clients' experiences, emotions, and attachment to their fixed ideas.

...on the experiential establishment...

ACT is an experiential approach. It can be so easy for clients, as well as therapists, to get stuck inside their heads. Just talking the entire session may not be much different than what clients are already doing with their thinking all day long. Having a different experience is important to get beyond thinking and old habits. Like anything else, you can overuse experiential exercises and techniques, or use them in a forced or artificial way, but when they are done with the right timing, they can really help clients experience a breakthrough.

...of greater psychological flexibility...

Clients often get stuck because they are not flexible in how they do things or how they respond to situations. Psychological flexibility means that you have the ability to persist when it is important to persist, and that you can change what you are doing when what you are doing is not working (Biron & Veldhoven, 2012; Gloster, Klotsche, Chacker, Hummel, & Hoyer, 2011; Moran, 2013). That's flexibility—knowing when to change, and when to persist. If we can help clients do that, they become much better equipped to lead more fulfilling lives.

...primarily through acceptance, defusion, establishment of a transcendent sense of self, contact with the present moment, values, and building larger and larger patterns of committed action linked to those values.

ACT uses six processes to foster psychological flexibility: acceptance, defusion, self-as-context, mindfulness, values, and committed action. Each of these processes will be discussed in more detail, and an entire chapter will be devoted to each.

Now, here is a short definition of ACT:

A Short Definition of ACT

ACT uses acceptance and mindfulness processes, and commitment and behavior change processes, to produce greater psychological flexibility.

—*Steven C. Hayes, contextualscience.org*

So, in a nutshell, if you're flexible, you're going to be able to take action to do the things that matter to you. If you practice acceptance and mindfulness processes, you become less caught up in battling your own thoughts and emotions, leaving you more energy to take steps toward the things that you value in life.

Now you have the big picture of what ACT is all about. You may be confused, but we are going to go back over those concepts in a lot more detail as we go along. It is often good to sit with confusion— it allows you to set aside preconceived ideas, providing an opening into unexplored territory.

To put the six essential ACT processes in context, let's first explore the foundational principles of ACT in more detail.

FUNCTIONAL CONTEXTUALISM

As mentioned earlier, context and function are very important things to consider. For example, below is a picture of a bucket full of holes.

Many people would see a bucket with holes in it like this and say, "That bucket is broken. It's completely useless. Let's throw it in the trash can." However, can you think of a time when you might want to have a bucket with holes in it? When I ask this question to my workshop audiences, I get some pretty interesting responses, like:

- A watering pot for your garden
- A camp shower
- A strainer
- A candle holder to project star-like light onto the walls

If the context and function of the bucket is to carry water from one place to another, it may be useless if it has holes in it. However, in different contexts, the bucket can serve very useful functions.

This is really important, because clients may say, "I'm broken. There's nothing good about me. My anxiety is horrible. I'm useless." But you know what? It's likely that their anxiety and their behaviors served a useful function in a different context, so we can't automatically define any one specific behavior as good or bad. We always have to pay close attention to the context of the behavior and the function it serves.

Likewise, **be careful not to automatically label anxiety and avoidance behaviors as bad.** In the context of being confronted by a hungry bear while out in the wilderness, their anxiety will function to get them ready to run away, and avoidance will save their lives. If they do not feel anxiety, they might not be motivated to escape, and they will be eaten.

If a client has been hurt by other people in the past, they may feel anxiety now when they are around strangers. The anxiety was functioning to protect the client in the past, but in the context of going out shopping, the anxiety and avoidance makes it difficult for the client to get their groceries.

Understanding this, clients can see that **anxiety itself is not necessarily the enemy**, so they can begin to change their relationship with it.

THE POWER AND PROBLEMS OF LANGUAGING

RFT is a very well-researched scientific approach to languaging, which refers to how words acquire meaning, associations, and emotions (Torneke, Barnes-Holmes, & Hayes, 2010). RFT is very important, providing a scientific foundation for the ACT processes. RFT is to ACT like an engine is to a car. You can drive a car and have no idea how the engine works, though knowing how engines work can make you a better driver, and will be helpful if engine problems come up. Likewise, understanding RFT can make you a better therapist, though you don't necessarily have to understand how RFT works to use ACT.

Language is a very powerful tool that human beings have developed. Language helps us to describe, evaluate, and problem solve. This is extremely useful for external problems. If I see a large furry creature with sharp teeth, that description can help identify a lion. I then evaluate that the lion is dangerous, because I have seen it eat my friends. And then I problem solve, perhaps deciding to climb a tree, because I have never seen a lion climb a tree. In this case, language has literally saved my life. This is why language is such a powerful thing, and why we humans use it so much.

However, problems arise when we start to get lost in language itself as if it's a real thing, rather than a representation of reality. If I describe myself as someone with an unfulfilling job, no friends, and overwhelming anxiety, I might evaluate myself as a complete loser. I might then problem solve by engaging in self-harming behaviors, isolating myself, or staying away from people. **The same process of language ends up being a very unhelpful thing when I use it against myself, and I forget that these things are literally just words.**

We are not born with language. Babies don't think in words. As they grow up, babies hear the people around them talking, so they start to imitate that talk. As they learn it, they start to internalize that language, and they start saying things to themselves. Thinking is just sub-vocal conversation with yourself. Isn't it weird that we spend so much of our lives thinking in words? Don't you know what you're going to say to yourself? Why do you have to say it to yourself, and then talk back to yourself?

When you think to yourself, you consider what you want to say, and then you put that thought into words. Then you tell yourself these words, and then you've got to remember what those words mean so you will know what it is that you meant to tell yourself. Isn't it bizarre that we spend so much time doing this? We forget that we ourselves give these words meaning and power. Though they are designed to represent things and concepts, they are nothing more than sounds. They have no meaning and no power in and of themselves.

For example, if I were to say right now, *Anata wa baka desu,* unless you happen to speak Japanese, all you would probably hear is "blah, blah, blah, blah, blah." But if I were to say it in English, "You're stupid," do you sense how those words have power? Those words have been conditioned with meanings and associations. However, if you didn't speak English, you probably wouldn't feel anything in particular. You wouldn't have any upsetting emotions, and you wouldn't have any memories associated with them. They would literally just be sounds. **We give words meaning, then forget we do it, and then we get upset about those sounds.**

Clients have thoughts in their heads, like "I'm stupid," and then they try to problem solve those sounds, and often end up doing things that are very unhealthy. They forget that those are just sounds, or representations of sounds in their heads, and that they have no meaning other than what their brains give them.

Of course, thinking can be a very useful tool for solving problems in the external world. Thinking itself is not a bad thing. Problems arise when we forget that thoughts are just symbols, and we act as if they are real. We waste a lot of time and energy fighting and arguing with symbols.

Take the word "tree." There is no such thing as a tree. That word is a conceptualization. There are different types of trees, and they all look a little different. Different people will think of different types of trees when they hear the word. Using words can be a very convenient thing, but we can forget that the word "tree" is only a symbol, a kind of shorthand. We can get caught up in mental images, instead of actually appreciating the reality of pine cones, maple leaves, or the trunk of an oak.

Likewise, the word "anxiety" is a symbol. There is no such thing as "anxiety" in the real world. Everyone will have a slightly different experience when they use the word anxiety. They may have heart palpitations, churning feelings, light-headedness, tension in their necks, and other experiences, and then they label those sensations with the word "anxiety." Then, **they forget that anxiety is a label, and fight the label, rather than relating to the physical reality of what they are experiencing in their bodies.**

Growing up, a lot of our education involves words, so words become a huge, central focus in our lives. We can begin to confuse our thoughts with reality, and can lose touch with our physical senses.

The process of cognitive defusion, which we will discuss later, can help us get back in touch with these distinctions.

Because language can be so powerful, we can also leverage it as a tool in therapy. In ACT, it is common to use metaphors, in which we use language and imagery to get beyond linear thinking. If you can find the right metaphors, you can wake up a more visceral experience for a client. For example, instead of saying, "Running away from your anxiety just keeps making it worse," you can ask, "Does it feel like you are caught in a hamster wheel? That the faster you run, the more you tire yourself out, and you're just not getting anywhere?"

You will find a wide variety of metaphors throughout this workbook and in other books on ACT. There is also a wonderful collection of metaphors in *The Big Book of ACT Metaphors* (Stoddard & Afari, 2014). Once you get ACT, you can even spontaneously make up creative metaphors specific to the client in front of you, especially when you find the session becoming rote and the dialogues superficial. Sometimes, our clients are able to express their own metaphors about their experiences (and they often express appreciation when I ask their permission to incorporate their metaphors into my own therapeutic toolbox to use with other clients).

THE REALITY OF SUFFERING

In ACT, **suffering is considered a normal human experience**. It is a natural part of being alive. We are not going to pretend that suffering doesn't exist, or that we can be happy all the time. This is not a realistic goal. If you want to have good relationships, you are going to sometimes get hurt when you feel rejected, or you will be distraught when something happens to your loved ones. If you want to learn and grow, you are going to sometimes make mistakes and fail. This is the richness of living life fully.

In the Eastern wisdom traditions, there are teachings that describe attachment as the cause of suffering. Some people misinterpret this to mean that you shouldn't get involved in relationships, or that you shouldn't have material possessions. However, as we know from the most basic laws of physics, everything is always changing. Since you can't hold on to things that are changing all the time, the attempt to try to hold on and keep something from changing is going to cause suffering for you. The mental attempt to try to keep everything exactly the same creates suffering, because it is impossible to do. You do not need to forego things and relationships—in fact, you can appreciate them all the more in this moment knowing that everything is impermanent. For example, if you try to keep your kids from growing up, everyone will suffer. But if you keep in the back of your mind that they will only be this age once, it reminds you to make time to be present with them and enjoy them as they are now.

It is not a good idea to wait until all your suffering is gone before you live your life. A lot of therapists target clients' suffering, perhaps going back to the medical model. If you go to a medical doctor with a problem, you want that problem fixed, or the pain taken away. But suffering, especially the emotional kind, is a part of life. You can't take it out of life. If you are going to live, then suffering is going to come with that sometimes.

This is a really important aspect of ACT—it does not focus on symptom reduction. Other approaches focus on trying to get rid of anxiety, or on trying to get rid of thoughts you don't like. Clients can end up spending their entire lives trying to get rid of anxiety and anxious thoughts, not realizing that it is like trying to have up without down, or a back without a front. ACT does not get caught up in that struggle—it focuses on making life more fulfilling.

By the way, we are not so inhuman as to say that if you're suffering, and there is a way to fix it, that you shouldn't do that. If you have a headache, we are not going to say you should feel that headache and accept that headache. If you can do something about it, like take an aspirin, then of course that could be helpful. But what if, for instance, you have a neurological condition and you've already gone through the surgery, and they just can't do much for the pain, or you've tried the meds and the pain is there anyway? Can you let go of the struggle with your own body, and find a way to live a fulfilling life even with the pain?

PSYCHOPATHOLOGY: WHAT GOES WRONG

Any good theory of therapy must have a model of psychopathology. In other words, what is it that makes things go wrong? As mentioned earlier, at the center of a wide variety of psychological problems lies inflexibility, or doing things that are not working and expecting a different result, or not persisting in doing something when that would help create a better life.

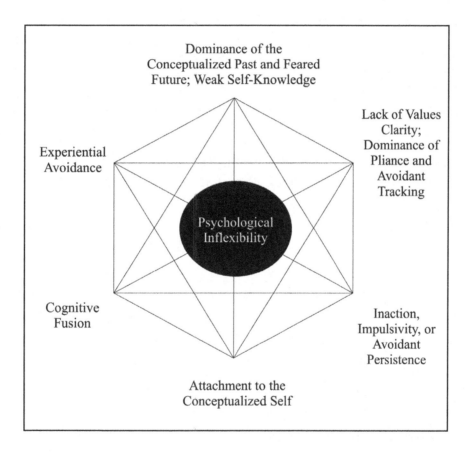

There are six unhelpful processes that contribute to this inflexibility: Attachment to the Conceptualized Self, Cognitive Fusion, Experiential Avoidance, Dominance of the Conceptualized Past and Future/ Limited Self-Knowledge, Lack of Values Clarity/Contact, and Unworkable Action (Hayes, Strosahl, & Wilson, 2012). These six are illustrated above as a hexagon, informally known as the "inflexahex," with lines connecting each one, because they all affect each other. Even though they are interdependent, it can be useful clinically to start to break these apart to talk about them.

The following handout explores these six areas in plain language, and gives clients a chance to consider the ways they have been engaging in processes that lead to inflexibility, which might be more simply described as feeling "stuck."

Ways We Get Stuck

If you struggle with anxiety, you know it leaves you feeling stuck, trapped in a vicious cycle. The bad news, as you have probably discovered, is that the cycle is self-perpetuating if you don't understand it. The good news is that modern research has discovered six processes that keep people stuck. Understanding these six problems is the first step toward moving out of the trap.

As best you can, consider exploring each of these six areas as learning opportunities, not as more ways to beat yourself up. These traps are common for all human beings, especially intelligent ones (so if you have been really stuck, you must be really smart!).

Forgetting Who You Really Are

The anxiety you have been struggling with can begin to feel like it has become your whole life. You might even define yourself as "an anxious person" to others. When you rigidly hold on to a fixed idea of who you are, you become stuck. After all, how can an anxious person live a fulfilling life? With all the anxiety and other problems you are dealing with, it can be hard to remember that you are so much more.

How have you been defining yourself in ways that keep you stuck?

_____

_____

_____

_____

Getting Stuck in Anxious Thoughts

Anxious thoughts can feel very powerful. They seem to get stuck in your head. The more you attempt to stop them, the more you try to control them, and the more you try to talk yourself out of them, the worse they tend to get. Even when you temporarily ignore them, they seem to keep creeping back into your mind. It is like we are lost in the movies of our minds, and we believe they are real. If you forget that a movie is just a projection, you feel very emotional about it. When you believe that the thoughts inside your head are real, and not just in your head, they can keep you stuck.

What strong thoughts have been keeping you stuck?

_____

_____

_____

_____

Trying to Avoid the Anxiety

By definition, anxiety is unpleasant. Nobody would want to feel anxiety if they didn't have to. So of course you have been working hard not to feel the anxiety.

Here's the problem. The feelings of anxiety are you. They are happening in your body. You might be able to distract yourself temporarily, but you can't avoid yourself forever. Anxiety is not an alien inside you that you have to get rid of. It is your body doing what it is designed to do. And as you may have noticed, **you can't run away from your own body.**

Since you can't run away from yourself, maybe you learned to avoid situations or places that might spark anxiety. The anxiety seems lower when you avoid those triggers. But what is the price you pay? Do you feel lonely? Do you feel like you don't have much of a life? Avoiding situations that might spark anxiety is not always possible, and the more you try to avoid, the worse the anxiety gets when you do try to get back out into those situations.

In what ways have you tried to control or avoid your anxiety? What situations or places do you avoid?

_____

_____

_____

_____

Lost in the Past and the Future, Out of Touch with Yourself

If you are feeling anxiety right now, you probably would rather be somewhere else in your head than be in this moment. But if you spend most of your life in the past and the future, you're going to feel stuck, because this moment is the only time you will ever be able to take action and live your life.

Also, when you are living mostly in your head, you don't notice as much about yourself.

I certainly wish there was someone who could come along and fix everything for you, but no one will be able to know you as well as you. You might not like what you find, but it will be very important to investigate your own thoughts, emotions, and behaviors to discover the places in which you are stuck.

In what ways do you run away from yourself? How much time do you spend living in your head? How much do you think about the past and the future?

_____

_____

_____

_____

Losing Touch with What Really Matters to You

You will also feel stuck if your life seems to have no meaning or purpose. If all of your attention is focused on your problems and on your anxiety, it will not seem like much of a life, so you will not be motivated to do things differently.

You might also feel that you have been living someone else's life, following the expectations of your parents, friends, coworkers, or society. You have been doing what good people are supposed to do. But somehow, even though that was supposed to make you happy, you feel unfulfilled. Maybe people gave you the impression that life is supposed to be full of anxiety, so you didn't realize things could be different.

In what ways have you lost touch with what matters most? Who or what have you been living for?

_____

_____

_____

_____

Fruitless Efforts

No one can call you lazy. You have worked really, really hard to get rid of your anxiety. But do you feel like you are spinning your wheels, or banging your head against a brick wall? Maybe you've also tried giving up, but that hasn't helped either. It sure seems like the things you are doing should work, but they haven't.

But what if the cards are stacked against you? It may be that the very things you are doing are keeping you stuck. If you keep doing the same things over and over again, you can't expect a different result.

What have you been doing that might actually be keeping you stuck?

_____

_____

_____

_____

Later, you will work with your therapist on how to get unstuck in each of these six areas, but the first step is to become more aware of what is keeping you stuck. Go over this worksheet several times over the next week to allow yourself to fully digest this. We are often so lost in the feeling of being stuck that we cannot see the trap we are in. It is important to take some time to better understand that trap.

THE HEXAFLEX

There are six processes in ACT to undo the six problems that create inflexibility (Hayes, Luoma, Bond, Masuda, & Lillis, 2006; Hayes, Strosahl, & Wilson, 2012). This has been called the ACT hexagon. Since flexibility is in the center, it has also been called the hexaflex. In the diagram, lines connecting each process to all the others remind us that they are interdependent. Each one affects all the others. However, it can be useful clinically to separate these out. Remember that these are processes, not techniques. We can use a wide variety of techniques in the service of increasing psychological flexibility for clients—and these are helpful for therapists too! (Luoma & Vilardaga, 2013).

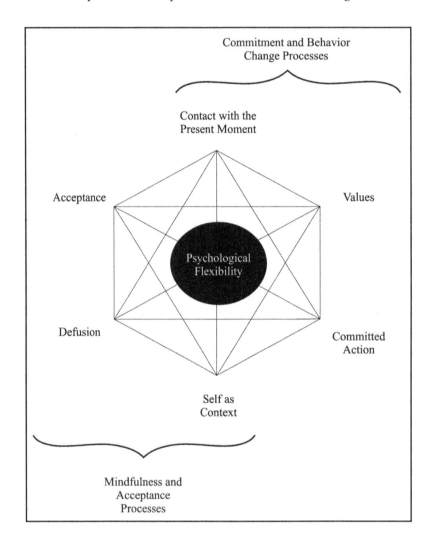

The four processes on the left are considered mindfulness and acceptance processes. The four on the right are commitment and behavior change processes. Notice that self as context and contact with the present moment belong to both. We have to be present and in touch with a bigger sense of who we are to be in the moment and to make changes.

Each of these six processes will be discussed in detail in the chapters that follow. In the following handout, an overview of these six processes are summarized in plain language to help clients get a big picture of what the ACT approach is all about.

ACT to Get Unstuck

Once you see the things that are keeping you stuck in the anxiety trap, how do you break the cycle? Researchers have identified six processes that can help. How you use these processes will depend on your specific situation, but let's look at the big picture.

Connecting to a Bigger You

Instead of identifying yourself with your anxiety, you can practice remembering that you are a whole lot more than your anxiety. You may have a lot of problems, but you are not your problems. You may have anxious thoughts, but you are not your thoughts. You may have anxious feelings, but you are not your feelings. You are the one having those experiences. If you can have thoughts, emotions, or problems, you must be bigger than them.

You are more than anything you can say you are in words. You may be a child, a parent, a sibling, an employee, an athlete, a partner, and play all kinds of other social roles. Yet, there is a bigger you that has learned to play all these roles.

You also have a history. You were once a baby, a child, a teenager, a young adult. There is a thread that connects all those yous, a bigger sense that has witnessed the experiences that have occurred over all those years. That you is much more than the anxiety you are feeling right now.

When you remember that you are much more than anxiety, you become less stuck in it.

Thoughts Are Not Reality

The word "water" represents a liquid reality, but you can't drink the word "water." A menu represents food, but you can't eat it. Likewise, our thoughts can be useful to represent reality, but they are actually only sounds inside our heads.

With practice, you can learn to recognize that your thoughts are just thoughts. Sometimes they are useful, but there is no need to fight with them. After all, if you argue with yourself, who are you going to win against?

When you learn to let go of the battle with your own thoughts, you free up a lot of energy to engage with more important things.

Acceptance of Reality and Your Feelings

Your anxiety has probably created a lot of problems in your life. It has likely robbed you of a lot of opportunities. I'll bet it's had a big impact on your work and your relationships. It's not fair. You don't deserve this. It shouldn't be this way.

That is all true, but unfortunately, wishing things were different hasn't changed anything. The reality right now is that you suffer from anxiety.

We waste a great deal of effort and energy fighting reality. When we learn to accept reality as it is, we free up a lot of energy, and become more flexible in how we deal with things.

This reality may include feelings of anxiety. A lot of us are taught, "I can't feel that way. I've got to distract myself. I've got to fight it." You probably wouldn't scream at a child or a friend for having anxiety. It's a natural feeling. Anxiety comes with being human. You can learn to let yourself have the anxiety, even if it is uncomfortable, if it is already here anyway. You don't have to fight or try to control your own emotions all the time.

You may not like the emotions you are having, or reality as it is, but it is hard to deal effectively with reality if you do not accept it.

Awareness in this Moment

Contact with the present moment, or mindfulness, is essential to getting unstuck. The moment you are in—right here, right now—is the only time that you are ever going to be able to experience anything or to take action. However, a lot of us live in our heads, off somewhere in the future or in the past. While that can sometimes be useful, to live a fulfilling life, we need the ability to be present in our experiences. To work with challenging situations, we need to bring our attention to our senses, thoughts, feelings, and habits. Just as we can strengthen our muscles through physical exercise, we can strengthen our attention and presence with mindfulness exercises.

In a very real sense, this moment is all that exists, so it's an important place to be. Everything else is only in your mind.

Keep in Mind What Really Matters

What is important to you? What really matters in your life? What is your anxiety getting in the way of?

Anxiety can seem so huge, and our problems can seem so big, that they become the focus of our lives. While our problems can definitely be important, if we lose perspective, we forget what life is really about. Getting in touch with your values means connecting with what is important to you. Of course, no one can tell you what your life values should be. You need to find out for yourself, or perhaps rediscover it for yourself.

If you have a "why," or if you have a reason to change things, you will be more willing to do the work.

Committed Action

This may sound obvious, but if you want things to be different, you have to do something different. Just thinking about it is not enough. Once you know where you want to go, it is important to set goals to get there. People sometimes talk about change for years, and no change ever happens. Action is needed to make changes in one's life.

Because big changes can seem daunting, you can begin with small, concrete steps that take you toward what matters, even if you are feeling anxious. If you value health, you can go take a five-minute walk. If you value family, you can write a note telling a loved one something you appreciate about them.

If you tell yourself, "I'm going to get rid of all my anxiety first, and then I'm going to live my life," you might just run out of lifetime before that ever really happens. Just take one small step at a time.

The ACT Question

Psychologist Steven Hayes encapsulates all of the above processes in a single question: "Given a distinction between you and the stuff you struggle with, are you willing to have that stuff, fully and without defense, as it is and not what it says it is, AND do what takes you in the direction of your chosen values, at this time, in this situation?"

Contemplating this question regularly can help you become more flexible in how you approach life, which will be an important ingredient as you create a life worth living.

In the remaining chapters, we will explore each one of the six ACT processes in more detail. I will also provide experiential exercises for both you and your clients so you can develop a deeper understanding of what these six processes are about. Let's begin by learning how to set up our values compass to lead us toward a life worth living.

Chapter 2

Setting Your Life Course: Does Anxiety Drive Your Life?

Values are a very important component of ACT. Anxiety, by definition, is unpleasant, so no one would willingly choose to feel it or work with it directly without a good reason. This chapter is designed to help clients identify and clarify what is most important for them in their lives. Without a sense of purpose or meaning, clients will not be as willing to engage in the difficult work of therapy.

Unfortunately, many clients become so caught up in fighting and avoiding their feelings of anxiety that they do not put much thought into what really matters to them. This chapter will provide exercises and worksheets to help reawaken the creative parts of clients that may have been long dormant. When dealing more directly with anxiety in the chapters that follow, clients will be asked to keep in mind what is really important to them to give them motivation to become more flexible.

Tip for Clinicians

Because they cause our clients so much turmoil, we can get overly focused on their distressing thoughts, emotions, and problems. While we may sometimes need to help them problem solve, we can end up getting pulled into their never-ending cycle of struggle. Reminding them (and ourselves) of what really matters keeps their awareness on the big picture, and can inspire them to do the difficult work of therapy.

LACK OF VALUES CLARITY/CONTACT

From an ACT perspective, lack of values clarity or contact leads to psychological inflexibility. In other words, if you are not clear about what is important to you, or not in touch with what matters to you, you're not going to be flexible in your behavior. Without values, clients may feel ungrounded. If all they are doing is fighting their problems, and life is meaningless, they will feel there is no point in taking steps toward change, and they develop a "Why bother?" attitude. It is important to help clients to connect to what really matters to them.

Stephen Covey (1989) talks about differentiating "urgent" from "important." In my emergency medical technician training, this was crucial to learn. Seeing blood at an accident scene seemed urgent, but if the patient was not breathing, or there was no heartbeat, the bleeding was not important. Patching up a minor cut would be a distraction from getting the heart beating again and could in fact cost the patient their life. Likewise, clients can spend their time fighting with what feels like urgent thoughts and anxious feelings, forgetting to focus on what they want their lives to be all about. While they are ruminating and avoiding, they are not engaging with what matters.

The accompanying handout highlights the problems that arise when one's life lacks direction, and is based on the classic "bus metaphor" (Hayes, Strosahl, & Wilson, 2012).

Who's Driving, and Where Do You Want to Go?

ACT uses a metaphor called "the passengers on the bus." The bus represents your life, and you are the driver. As this bus has been going along through the course of your lifetime, you have been taking on a lot of passengers: life experiences, thoughts, memories, and emotions. While some of these passengers are very pleasant, and we enjoy having them on our bus, some are downright monstrous, scary, and smelly. They don't do what we want them to do. They are unruly. Here we are driving our bus, and all these monsters are screaming and yelling, throwing spit wads at our heads, and generally creating a ruckus.

Because these passengers are so annoying, many people stop driving and pull the bus over to the side of the road to give them a lecture, or to fight these monsters. People spend a great deal of time and energy trying to wrestle them off the bus. But for better or for worse, these passengers are a part of you, a part of your history, so you can't get them off the bus. Because you don't like them and they make you so uncomfortable, you keep trying to push them off the bus, and your bus ends up going nowhere.

Or, because these monsters are so scary, you try to make secret deals with them. For example, let's say you want to do something that is important to you, like having a more fulfilling career. When you start to drive toward a more fulfilling career, the anxiety monster will rear its head and say, "Don't go that way! That makes us really uncomfortable!" Well, because you don't like that anxiety monster showing up, you just decide that you are not going to do anything that might make it upset. The secret deal is that if you keep your life small, the anxiety monster will keep quiet. But that silence comes at a price, and the price you pay is not being able to live a fulfilling life.

To keep from going in circles your whole life, **you need to decide where you want to go**. Do you want the anxiety to drive? Do you want these thoughts to steer? Thoughts and feelings can be pretty fickle and unpredictable. Do you want those to actually drive your bus, or do you want to drive your own bus, even if all those passengers have to come along for the ride? If having a more fulfilling career is important to you, just go that way. Let the monsters yell. Let them scream. Let them throw their spit wads. You will be doing what matters to you, even if the monsters don't like it.

Guess what? If you first think you can completely clean up your bus, you may never get around to driving your life where you want it to go. In fact, while you're stopped or going in circles, other passengers keep getting on—maybe loneliness, guilt, regret, and more anxiety. Get behind the wheel, decide where you want to go, and push the gas pedal. If the monsters get rowdy, don't fight with them. Just say, "Come on all you dear monsters, my old friends, we're going for a ride!"

Of course, it may be that you've been fighting for so long that you don't really know where you want to go. Use the worksheets throughout this chapter to help you connect to what really matters to you.

VALUES

If you think about the clients you've had who have done the best, I bet they had some bigger reasons, some bigger purpose or value that inspired them to go through that difficult stuff.

If you are a licensed mental health professional, you likely went to graduate school. If I had described to you exactly what graduate school was, would that have sounded like a fun thing to do? "Hey, have I got a deal for you! You give me so much money you could have bought a house with it, and I'll give you lots of stress, sleepless nights, and you're not going to eat very well. Oh, and you're going to be evaluated constantly, and will be repeatedly told about all the things you're doing wrong. You might even lose a few significant relationships along the way, because people just won't understand why you want to spend so much time doing this grad school thing instead of spending more time with them. At times, you will have lots of unpleasant emotions, like anxiety, fear, and hopelessness, and you will have thoughts about quitting and doubts about yourself and your ability to finish the program. And at the end of it all, you get to take an exam, and if you can't pass it, you will have wasted all that time and money. What do you say? Does that sound like a good deal?" Well, even if there were times you didn't want to continue, you endured all that stuff because you had the bigger value of wanting to live the glamorous lifestyle of a mental health professional. (Why does everyone always laugh when I say that?)

Hopefully, you found some fun along the way too, but I think you get my point. You were willing to be uncomfortable, were willing to be evaluated, and were willing to jump through all the hoops because there was a bigger reason for you to do it.

Being in touch with what really matters to you, and knowing you can take steps toward it, increases your willingness to do the work of therapy. If you have a reason to do so, you will be more willing to do things you might not enjoy doing, and to have uncomfortable feelings and distressing thoughts rather than getting lost in struggling with them.

Tip for Clinicians

Make sure you stay in touch with your own values, both for your career and for your life. When a client seems particularly challenging, remind yourself of your bigger value of helping others through those challenges, and the ripple effects that happen all around an individual when they do better. For those days when everyone seems challenging, remind yourself of all the other things that make your life meaningful besides being a therapist.

It can be helpful to incorporate the values process of ACT into any other treatment that you are already doing. Help clients figure out what matters to them. Why would they even want to be working on any of their problems? What are their symptoms getting in the way of?

Values are like compass headings. They give your life direction, but you can never arrive there. If going east is important to you for some reason, you never arrive at "east," you just move in that direction. Values remind you of the direction you want your life to go.

For example, family is one of my values. I can never say "I've accomplished the goal of family," check that box, and say I'm "done" with family. Family will be important to me throughout my entire life. I will continue to do things that move me in the direction of having a closer relationship with family. I will never arrive. It is the journey that I value.

Of course, we do also need to set specific goals to take us in the direction of our values, as we will discuss in chapter 8. If a value of mine is family, then I can set the concrete goals of going on dates with my wife and playing with my children. It is important to set goals. Those goals can also shift over time as circumstances change. However, goals are useless without values or a clear direction.

Tip for Clinicians

Be careful not to project your own values onto your clients, or try to talk them into what you feel is important. They may come from different backgrounds, different cultures, and have different life experiences, and therefore have totally different values. Our job is to help them get more in touch with their own values. Also, don't push clients for extravagant values that change the world, like becoming the doctor that cures cancer. In a very real sense, the humble goal of spending more time with family can change the world. Adding a little more love and reducing a little turmoil can have ripple effects.

Sometimes clients confuse rules with values, or get caught up in what they "should" do, based on society, parents, or old assumptions. We feel "pulled" to engage with our real values, rather than feeling "pushed" to do it. If a client's attitude is "Well, I guess I ought to spend more time with my family," that's probably not a value. That's probably something they are doing out of a sense of duty (although duty can be a value), or because somebody else thinks they should. When you connect to a real value, you have a sense of "I want more of this in my life. This is what I want to spend my time doing."

Ten Categories of Values

The Valued Living Questionnaire lists 10 major categories of values (Wilson, Sandoz, Kitchens, & Roberts, 2010). For some clients, it can be useful to just go over these general domains to open up the process of exploration. Interestingly, the first four out of the ten categories involve relationships (family, romantic, parenting, and friendships). Although some clients, such as individuals on the autism spectrum, may not put relationships on the top of their values list, the vast majority of human beings place at least some degree of value on relationships.

For some clients, their careers or employment is what brings them fulfillment. For others, education, or personal growth and development, gets them inspired (which is what you are doing right now!).

Another category is recreation, fun, or leisure. It really is sad to see the response I often get when I ask clients, "What do you do for fun, or what hobbies do you have?" Many of them literally stare at me blankly. "Fun, what do you mean, fun? I don't have any fun. All I do is wake up, feed the kids, go to work, come home, feed the kids, and go to bed. That's my life!" To which I typically reply, "Well, is that the life you want?" A lot of us are taught that only when all the work is done can we have some fun. Unfortunately, **your life may be over before all the work is done**. I encourage you to ask your clients (and yourself!) to ponder, "What is fun or enjoyable for you, and how can you add a little bit more of that into your life?"

The other day I went to a hobby shop with my youngest daughter, and I saw model rockets for sale. When I was a kid, I always wanted a Mercury Redstone rocket, but I could never afford one with my 50-cent allowance. So, I bought one that day. I took it home, cut up the balsa wood, put it together, painted it, and shot it up at the local park. Many people in today's society need to do more activities like that—things that have nothing to do with paying bills or being productive. It doesn't have to take a lot of time or money, but it can have a big impact on our quality of life.

Spirituality is a category that is very important for some clients. Many therapists have been taught to avoid discussing this, but by not ever bringing it up, we can be downplaying a very important aspect of clients' lives (Sears & Niblick, 2014). Of course, we can define spirituality very broadly. Even pure science can be spiritual in the sense of feeling amazement that here we are, that these atoms, which were crushed together in exploding stars, assembled themselves into a being that can contemplate its own existence. However you interpret spirituality, for many clients, it is important to have a framework that gives life meaning.

Another category of values relates to citizenship, environment, and community, which is about having a sense of belonging to, and taking care of, something bigger than yourself. The last category of values is about health and physical well-being, which is very important to some clients, although many clients only do it because they think it's good for them. While it is good to exercise, pay attention to whether clients are doing something out of duty or because it is something they feel pulled and energized to do.

You can use the following worksheet to help clients explore these 10 domains.

Ten Domains of Values

When you're anxious, your mind can sometimes tell you that nothing matters, because you are so caught up in dealing with problems, or with what might go wrong. It can be easy to lose touch with what we really value in life. After all, the whole point of dealing with all of our problems is to make our lives more enjoyable.

Use this worksheet to open up that part of your brain that you may have lost touch with—that part of you that can feel joy, fulfillment, and excitement about living.

While there may be a nearly infinite variety of values, Kelly Wilson and colleagues created a Valued Living Questionnaire that identifies 10 broad areas (Wilson, Sandoz, Kitchens, & Roberts, 2010). Use these broad categories to start the process of rediscovering what really matters to you.

Read through each area below. Rate how important each area is to you on a scale of 1-10, with 1 being not important at all, and 10 being very important.

1. Family Relations. How important is this to you on a scale of 1-10? _____

Are there specific things about family that you value?

_____

_____

_____

2. Marriage/Couples/Intimate Relations. How important is this to you (1-10)? _____

Are there specific things about this area that you value?

_____

_____

_____

3. Parenting. How important is this to you (1-10)? _____

Are there specific things about parenting that you value?

_____

_____

_____

4. Friendships/Social Life. How important is this to you (1-10)? _____

Are there specific things about social life that you value?

_____

_____

_____

5. Career/Employment. How important is this to you (1-10)? _____

Are there specific things about this area that you value?

_____

_____

_____

6. Education/Personal Growth and Development. How important is this (1-10)? ____

Are there specific things about this area that you value?

_____

_____

_____

7. Recreation/Fun/Leisure. How important is this to you (1-10)? _____

Are there specific things about this area that you value?

_____

_____

_____

8. Spirituality. How important is this to you (1-10)? _____

Are there specific things about spirituality that you value?

_____

_____

_____

9. Citizenship/Environment/Community Life. How important is this (1-10)? _____

Are there specific things about this area that you value?

_____

_____

_____

10. Health/Physical Well-Being. How important is this to you (1-10)? _____

Are there specific things about physical well-being that you value?

_____

_____

_____

Now, look back over what you wrote. Do you notice any themes? Did anything in particular stand out to you? Did anything about this process surprise you?

_____

_____

_____

Go back through these questions several times over the next few weeks. Each time, you may be able to get more specific. For example, writing down "travel" is a good start, but where would you want to go? How long would the trip be? How often would you go to those places?

Sometimes it can be hard to distinguish what really matters to you, versus what you have been told by others should be important. Remember—no one can tell you what your values are. While it can be good to share certain values with our society and our culture, the goal is to determine what really makes your own life meaningful and worthwhile.

HELPING CLIENTS CONNECT WITH THEIR VALUES

Some clients know what really matters to them when they walk in the door, and those are our favorite clients, because they are motivated. Because they know what they want, they are willing to do the work. Other clients may work on values clarification for months, even years, because it's really hard for them to get at this. The first things they say may only be things that they think will sound good. You may have to spend some time helping them dive into what really matter to them.

It can be challenging for clients with anxiety to identify their values, because they are often so busy surviving that they don't engage with living. Do you remember the concept of mood-state dependent learning and memory (Ucros, 1989)? If you are in an anxious mood state, always focusing on problems, it can be hard to even think about what's fulfilling, meaningful, and useful.

Therefore, we may need to use some techniques (or tricks really) to help people get more in touch with the parts of their brains that connect with values. There are many ways to do this. The main principle is not so much to come up with the perfect value right away, but to just get the "juices flowing" at first by brainstorming. If you've ever been part of a brainstorming team, you know that it can be an amazing process, but only if people don't shut you down too quickly. If you throw out an idea, and someone else says, "That's a stupid idea!" that kills the creativity. What can happen is that a stupid idea leads to another stupid idea, which then leads to another stupid idea, which leads to a brilliant idea. You wouldn't have gotten to the brilliant idea had you not entertained the other ideas.

It can be the same with the process of getting more in touch with values. The initial point is to open up the mind to think more creatively about what is meaningful and what matters to them.

One way you can engage clients in a values discussion is to ask them about their childhood dreams. What did they want to be when they grew up? It doesn't necessarily matter what they say—what they wanted to be when they were kids is not necessarily going to be what they have to do. The point is to get some of the qualities of those dreams, whether or not they are even concrete or realistic, and to look for patterns. If a client says, "I wanted to be a hockey player when I was a kid, but that's a stupid dream!" you can reply with "Well what was it about being a hockey player that you found either fulfilling or interesting?"

On the other end of the life span, we can say, "Let's imagine that you could fast forward to the end of a long, meaningful life, whatever that means to you, and now you are at your funeral. By your definition, what would have been a life well lived? It doesn't necessarily have to be about accomplishments. What would you have wanted your life to have stood for? What would you want people to say about you?" (Once, when I asked that last question at a workshop, an audience member shouted, "Oh my God! He's come back to life!")

Or you could say something like, "Maybe you've had a near-death experience. If so, you probably remember feeling so lucky to be alive. It may have reset your life priorities. If you have not had a near-death experience, can you imagine what it would be like to believe you were going to die, but then realize that you were going to live? I have a friend who has cancer, and she was told she has only six months left to live. If that happened to you, what would you want to spend that time doing?" Such questions start to get at what is really important to clients.

Another way to get at values is to ask clients what they admire in other people or in their favorite movie characters. Use the following worksheet to explore qualities clients admire.

Superheroes or People You Admire

One way to get in touch with what you value is to consider the people you look up to or admire. Growing up, you probably had a relative, teacher, singer, movie star, or superhero that you admired or even wanted to be like. Perhaps those have changed since you have grown older, or perhaps you still admire those same people. What did or do you admire about them?

Superheroes stand for something, and believe in important things, like freedom, knowledge, health, and relationships. Superheroes come in all shape and sizes—take for example my daughter Caylee's creation, Waffleman.

Waffleman, as the story goes, was once just a regular young boy. He went to a costume party dressed as a waffle. Afterward, the zipper got stuck, and he could not remove the suit. He suddenly realized that he could shoot syrup through his fingers. At first, he was distraught, then he decided he could use his powers to help his friends and rescue people when they were attacked by covering the attacker with syrup. My daughter's friends admire this superhero because he turned adversity into an advantage, and is loyal and helpful to his friends.

Think of a superhero you like, or a person, living or dead, that you admire. Add as many names as you like to this list.

_____

_____

_____

_____

_____

_____

What qualities do they have? What do they value?

_____

_____

_____

_____

_____

_____

Which qualities and values would you like to have more of in your life?

_____

_____

_____

_____

_____

_____

Later, you can develop a plan and goals for getting more of what you value in your life, but the first step is getting more in touch with what really matters to you.

Magic Wands and Typical Days

In ACT, we aim to help clients live a more fulfilling life whether or not they have discomfort, distressing emotions and thoughts, or rough life circumstances. However, it can be difficult for clients to get in touch with values when their problems seem so overwhelming, so you can use the magic wand exercise from strategic therapy. "If I had a magic wand, and could take away any obstacles, what would you want more of in your life?"

Sometimes clients will answer that question with means rather than values, so don't be afraid to delve deeper. If a client says, "I just want to be rich," you can ask, "Okay. And if you were rich, what would you do?" If the answer is, "Well, I'd do whatever I want," you can respond with, "Well, what would you want to do? What would a typical day look like for you?"

The next two worksheets are designed to help clients dig deeper into what matters, and to help them consider how their daily lives would look if they were living their values.

And if You Had That, What Would That Give You?

When we are anxious, it can be challenging to get in touch with what it is that really makes life worth living. Setting time aside to explore our values can be very useful to get our lives on track to where we really want to go.

Years ago, I learned an exercise from my ninja teacher and mentor, Stephen K. Hayes. While we will use it to explore values, it was originally designed to create a meditative state beyond words. One person asks, "What do you want?" then keeps asking, "And if you had that, what even more important thing would that give you?" Even after starting with something mundane, like "a new car," the person being asked the question reaches a point where they answer with "freedom," "peace," or "love," and eventually words fail, leaving them with a bigger sense of what matters.

While you could certainly have a friend ask you these questions, and use it as a meditative exercise, for the worksheet below, we will use this exercise to get in touch with your values.

As you fill out this worksheet, watch what your mind does. Don't get too caught up in getting the "right" answers. Consider this an experiment. Don't rush to answer each question—you may choose to wait before answering, maybe even five or ten minutes. Sit in a quiet place, repeating the question to yourself, and see what bubbles up in your mind.

Begin by writing down something you want. It could be something major, or it could be something that may not seem very important. Be sure to write down something *you* want, not necessarily something that would impress others.

_____

_____

And if you had that, what even more important thing would that give you?

_____

_____

And if you had that, what even more important thing would that give you?

_____

_____

And if you had that, what even more important thing would that give you?

_____

_____

And if you had that, what even more important thing would that give you?

_____

_____

And if you had that, what even more important thing would that give you?

_____

_____

And if you had that, what even more important thing would that give you?

_____

_____

And if you had that, what even more important thing would that give you?

_____

_____

Continue asking yourself this question until you feel like you are hitting on what is really important to you.

Fill out this worksheet several times, perhaps once a day for a week or so. Interestingly, you might find that you get to the same answers even when you start with different initial wants. If so, you may be homing in on what really matters to you.

My Ideal Day

Sometimes we can get lost in ideas about what we want. We might automatically say we want things like health, wealth, relationships, and power, but what would you do with those things? Even if you had those things, what would your daily life look like?

As an exercise to get at what really matters, write out what your ideal day would be. Just to get the obstacles out of the way, imagine you don't have to worry about *how* to make it happen. Just think about what a perfect day for you would be. The point is not necessarily to strive to make this a reality, but to open up your mind to what is really important to you.

The point of this exercise is to better determine what **you** really would like your days to be like. Watch out for what might only be a reaction—if you were never allowed to do something, maybe you only want to do it to be contradictory. Or, your mind might be telling you things that sound good to others. Take some time to ask yourself what you really want.

As you write, go beyond things like "having no anxiety." If you had no anxiety, what would you be doing? Be as specific as you can. Instead of "spend time with family," how would you spend that time?

The practical side of your brain may do a lot of judging about what you write down, or throw out a lot of "yeah, buts." Just acknowledge that your brain is trying to help, and see if you can set those judgments aside for a little while. Just start writing. You can always edit later. In fact, you might wish to write this as a computer document so you can edit it as your ideas and feelings about what matters evolves and becomes clearer.

Use the prompts below to get started.

Where would you want to live?

_____

_____

_____

When would you wake up and what would you do first?

_____

_____

_____

How would you dress?

_____

_____

_____

What would your home be like?

_____

_____

_____

What meals would you eat?

_____

_____

_____

What activities would you do?

_____

_____

_____

What hobbies would you have?

_____

_____

_____

Who would you spend your time with?

_____

_____

_____

What would you do to relax?

_____

_____

_____

How would you end your day and when would you go to bed?

_____

_____

_____

How else would you describe your ideal day?

_____

_____

_____

Of all those things you have described in your ideal day, what is one thing you can do to make **today** a little bit more of an ideal day?

_____

_____

_____

When Clients Say They Don't Care

Since some clients have no idea what really matters to them, they may even become argumentative, saying things like, "I don't care about anything."

You can respond by saying, "Okay, notice that your brain is telling you that. I wonder if it's being influenced by some anxiety." One way to get at some of their values is to find out what they actually do, what they have done in the past, or what they would do if given a choice.

In this case, you might respond with, "Well, I noticed you got out of bed this morning. Why did you get out of bed this morning?"

"Well, I had to, because if I just stay in bed all the time, my mind will spin and my anxiety will grow, and they'll put me in the nut house."

"I see. So, it sounds like you value personal freedom. You value choice. You value being able to direct your own life. I also noticed that you came into my office today. Why didn't you just stay home and watch television all day?"

"Because my wife told me she is tired of me not dealing with my anxiety, and that I have to come."

"Okay, so it sounds like you value your relationship with your wife. I noticed that you have been talking with me today, when you could just sit there in silence the whole time and meet the requirement of just showing up."

"I guess I'm tired of living this way, and I want to get back to work."

"Maybe you felt like you were able to a make a difference when you were working, and lying in bed is not a very fulfilling way to live your life. If working is important to you, let's keep that in mind as we take some small steps to get you back to work."

You can get at some of these values by starting with what they are actually doing in their lives. It doesn't mean that's where you stop, but it can be a way of "priming the pump" to get them more in touch with what really matters.

Even the client's anxiety itself can provide clues about what matters to them, as we explore in the next worksheet.

Finding Your Values in Your Anxiety

When you feel overwhelmed by anxiety, it can be difficult to be in touch with your values, with what makes life worth living. However, hidden within your anxiety are clues about what is truly important in your life.

For example, if you have anxiety about getting sick, it likely means you value your health. If you worry a lot about your kids, they must give your life meaning. If you are worried about your partner, family, or friends, it likely means that you value those relationships.

Take a few moments to explore your anxiety to discover (or re-discover) some of your values. In the left column, write down things that create anxiety. Then, explore that anxiety to see if you can find something inside it that you value, and write the value(s) in the right column.

Anxiety	Value(s)
_____	_____
_____	_____
_____	_____
_____	_____
_____	_____
_____	_____

Now, here is the tough question. Would you be willing to have the anxieties in the left column if it means you get to have the values in the right column?

I'll bet your mind is saying, "No way! I don't want any anxiety!"

Yet, ironically, pushing the anxiety away has likely been also keeping the value away. It's like a two-sided coin, with anxiety on one side, and the value on the other. You can push or throw the coin away, but that comes with a cost. Hasn't your time spent fighting the anxiety cost you enough?

Of course, I'm not saying you have to suffer from anxiety for your whole life, but it is important to pay attention to the cost of pushing it away. Before you commit to doing the work of changing your life, it is important to get more in touch with what you truly value.

Tip for Clinicians ──

I am sometimes asked, "What if my clients have evil values, or ones that hurt other people?" In my experience, those are behaviors, not values. I believe that all human beings are trying to avoid suffering, and they sometimes do it in ways that cause harm. Perhaps they are hurting someone else to feel better about themselves, or perhaps their brains are wired to lack empathy. Perhaps they are causing harm because they want to make money. What is the value underneath making that money? Freedom to choose? A safe place to live? Help them find more productive and less harmful ways of moving toward those values.

Once clients know where they want to go, they have to stop driving in circles. The next chapter explores how we can help clients let go of what is not working.

Chapter 3

Letting Go of What Is Not Working

Even after clients identify what is important to them, they may end up continuing their old behaviors that have kept them stuck in their attempts to avoid their anxiety. They get trapped in automatic pilot modes of thinking, of emotionally reacting, and of behaving that temporarily reduce their anxiety but inadvertently make things worse in the long run. They often find themselves banging their heads into metaphorical brick walls, and when the walls do not give way, they hit their heads harder, and then complain that their heads hurt. Or, when paths open up, they stay "hunkered down," are unwilling to persist in moving forward.

This chapter helps clients systematically list and work through all the things they have attempted to do for their anxiety, with the purpose of helping them fully realize what has not been working. They come to realize that their attempts to control their thoughts and feelings contribute to the problems, not the solutions. This awareness helps them let go of old patterns, and fosters a sense of willingness to try something new for the sake of living a more fulfilling life. Our goal in doing this is to help the clients become more psychologically flexible.

PSYCHOLOGICAL FLEXIBILITY

Clients often come to us feeling stuck. The feeling of stuckness arises when things are rigid and inflexible. The opposite of stuckness is flexibility.

Psychological flexibility is defined as "contacting the present moment fully as a conscious, historical human being, and based on what the situation affords, changing or persisting in behavior in the service of chosen values" (Hayes, 2020).

Contacting the present moment fully is important, because **you can only be flexible in the here and now**. If you are somewhere else in your head, you are lost in the realm of thought. Being fully present involves engaging your senses in what you are experiencing in this moment.

You must also be conscious and mindful to be flexible. Zoning out or trying to escape into another state of consciousness makes it impossible to be flexible.

Part of being human involves having a history. There is a context to who you are, and your history is part of who you are in this present moment. A few years ago, I wrote an entire book on *The Sense of Self* (Sears, 2017b). I explored many different aspects of what it is that makes us feel like an independent self. In one chapter, I wrote about my work with neuropsychological testing. When I assessed individuals with neurocognitive disorders (dementia-like Alzheimer's Disease), I found that people without a history had great difficulty with psychological flexibility.

The second part of the definition of psychological flexibility—"based on what the situation affords"—refers to the importance of paying attention to context. How can you know what to do, and be flexible enough to choose wisely, if you are not aware of how the situation is unfolding from moment to moment?

Once we recognize the situation as it is, and we know what we value, we can decide if it will be best to persist in an important behavior, or to change what we are doing in order to move toward what really matters.

For example, think about the process of going to college or graduate school. In order to get your degree, I'll bet there were times you had to persist, even when you didn't want to. There were likely times you were tired and didn't feel like studying, or you didn't like a certain class, but you did the work anyway. Your wrists were hurting, but you finished that 15-page paper. You persisted because you had goals to take you toward that bigger value of becoming a professional. At other times in your training, I bet you had to change your behavior. Your supervisor said, "What you are doing is going to harm your clients. You need to not do that." You had to change your behavior in order to grow and in order to graduate.

How did you know when to persist and when to change your behavior? You had to pay attention in the present moment. You had to monitor your own performance. You had to be willing to receive and consider feedback from your professors and supervisors. I'll bet you had some classmates who did not persist, and/or did not change their behavior, and they probably did not graduate or get licensed. In order to move toward a long-term value, there are times when you need to change and times when you need to persist depending on the situation. That's what makes us flexible.

Clients with anxiety tend not to be very psychologically flexible. When they feel anxiety, they want to avoid the situations that might cause it, or distract themselves. When they become more flexible, they can still choose to avoid unpleasant situations, but they can also choose to feel the anxiety and go ahead and do the things that make their lives more meaningful.

Tip for Clinicians

Practice being psychologically flexible yourself. Watch out for your own rigidity in how you interact with your clients. Be aware of ideas you might be fused with. Be willing to be confused and to feel your own feelings, as you are asking the client to do.

The next worksheet explores the concept of psychological flexibility for clients.

Becoming More Flexible

The circumstances of our lives are constantly changing. Therefore, it is important to be flexible. Psychological flexibility has been shown to correlate with being mentally healthy. Being rigid and inflexible in your behaviors makes it more likely that you will struggle in life.

There are times we may need to persistently keep doing certain things, like going to work even when we don't feel like it. There are other times we need to change what we are doing, like yelling at people when it creates more anger and pushes people away. Flexibility is being able to decide which one is best to do, depending on the situation.

How do we know when to keep going, and when to change what we are doing? That requires paying attention to the effects of what you are doing. Use the questions below to get you started in examining how flexible you are.

Can you remember a time when you were able to persist, or keep going, and it helped you?

_____

_____

_____

_____

Can you remember a time when you gave up when it would have been better to keep going?

_____

_____

_____

_____

Can you remember a time when you realized what you were doing was not helping, and you changed what you were doing and got a better result?

_____

_____

_____

_____

Can you remember a time when you kept doing something that was not working, but you were unwilling or unable to change your behavior?

_____

_____

_____

_____

Are you doing anything now that has not been working, but you keep doing it anyway?

_____

_____

_____

_____

Is there anything now that you have given up on that you would like to do or have more of in your life now?

_____

_____

_____

_____

What is one small thing you can do today to move toward that?

_____

_____

_____

_____

The first step to creating change is to increase your awareness. Even if you don't like the answers you gave above, they will provide an important starting point toward making things different in your life.

CUTTING OUR LOSSES

It can be very difficult to let go of old habits. When you suggest to clients that they need to stop doing something, they may adamantly reply, "But I've always done it that way!" People invest so much into doing things a certain way that that they don't want to believe it doesn't work, because it means they will have wasted so much time and energy.

It's like the old joke about the person who is intoxicated looking for his lost car keys under the streetlamp because the lighting is better there. When he doesn't find them, he looks harder, rather than changing the place he looks. Likewise, people with anxiety may only work on their anxiety when they are safe at home, and they keep doing the same things with more effort, rather than getting out and going other places.

It is sad for people to acknowledge that they have wasted time and resources, especially since life is so brief and resources are limited. However, sometimes the best thing we can do is "cut our losses."

Tip for Clinicians

If a client says, "But I always do that!" don't argue with them. "Well, you are welcome to keep doing that. But let me ask you—has it made your life more fulfilling or less fulfilling? How has it worked, and what have the costs been?"

ACT uses two important metaphors to get at how struggling and continuing unhelpful behaviors can make things worse (Hayes, Strosahl, & Wilson, 2012), which are described in the next handout.

Caught in Quicksand and Trapped in a Hole

Sometimes people seem to blame you for your problems, but they have no idea how hard you've been working. Yet, **do you ever feel like the more you try, and the harder you work, the worse things get?**

Maybe it feels like you are caught in quicksand. Comedian John Mulaney once said that when he was a kid, he believed that one of the biggest dangers adults faced in life was quicksand. While that is not literally true, maybe you can relate to what it might feel like.

If you fall into a quicksand pit, the more you try to fight it, struggle with it, and get out of it, the more it sucks you under. So, what can you do? The best thing is to increase the surface area of your body. If you actually open up and lay back and spread your body out, more of your body is in contact with the sand, and you can "float" on the sand.

Isn't that the opposite of the gut reaction you would have in the middle of this dangerous situation? Your impulse might be to fight it in a desperate attempt to get out of the quicksand. Yet, if you spread out, then you can almost kind of swim over the top. Ironically, it is the struggle that sucks you under. In a lot of ways, **your battles with your own thoughts and anxiety can end up being similar to being trapped in quicksand.** If you are constantly struggling and fighting with what's going on with your own internal experiences, you may feel like you are drowning. It may seem scary, but if you are willing to just let go of the struggle, you may just end up floating with your experiences, even if they don't go away, and you can use your energy to swim toward what matters to you.

Maybe you can relate to another analogy. Imagine you are walking through a field on a dark, moonless night, and you fall into a deep hole. It is pitch black down there, and you can't see a thing. As you feel around, you find a shovel.

What's a shovel good for? Digging! Well, since you want to get out of there, you start digging. When you don't seem to be getting anywhere, you dig harder. Maybe you even try to dig steps in the sides of the hole, but it just makes the dirt collapse. The more scared and desperate you get, the harder you dig, not realizing that what you are doing is actually making things worse.

If I was at the top of that hole, I would shout down to you, "Stop that! Your digging is making it worse!" But if you had been working really hard, it's possible that you might say, "You don't understand! Nobody else is helping me. I'm down here all alone! I'm working as hard as I can, and nobody gives me credit for all the hard work I'm doing!"

Yet, the sad thing is that the hard work that you are doing is just digging the hole deeper and deeper and deeper. If I were to drop a ladder down to you and say, "Here, use this!" you might even grab the ladder, and try to dig with it. "Hey! This ladder doesn't help me at all! You're not trying to help. You're making it worse! This doesn't dig very well at all!"

What would you have to do? In this silly example, it would be obvious that you would need to drop the shovel. But if digging is all you had ever done, it would be scary to have to drop the shovel. You might be tempted to keep telling yourself that if you dig harder, you're eventually going to be successful. **But if you keep doing the same thing, you can't expect a different result.**

If you have worked really hard and struggled with anxiety all your life, it will be scary to stop what you've been trying to do, because you don't know what else to do.

Are you willing to drop the shovel? You may not yet know what else to do, but I can tell you that if you keep digging this hole, it's not going to help you live a more fulfilling life. Even if you don't know for sure what to do next, or how to get there, are you willing to let go of the shovel? Are you willing to be a little confused, anxious, or even scared, if it means you can get away from being stuck and move toward the life you want to live?

CREATIVE HOPELESSNESS

Creative hopelessness is the process of helping clients let go of what is not working (Hayes, 2007; Hayes, Strosahl, & Wilson, 2012). While the expression may sound negative, if we can evoke feelings of hopelessness in the client about the things that are not working for them, they are more likely to stop engaging in those behaviors. In fact, the point of this process is to help clients feel more hopeful that they can break out of the feeling of being stuck.

We could also call this "workability." In order for clients to become more flexible, they have to stop doing what has not been working. Though it sounds obvious, if you do what you have always done, you will get what you have always got.

When using the technique of creative hopelessness, we want to find out what the client has already tried, and what has not worked for them. Clients often want to keep doing what they have always done, somehow expecting a different result. Clients may literally say to you, "I'm working so hard! Nobody knows how hard I'm working!"

You may have clients who are metaphorically banging their heads against the wall. You calmly say, "Well, maybe you shouldn't bang your head against the wall." The clients then say, "You don't understand! I'm working so hard trying to break through this wall. I'm really persevering with this! You're not being helpful by telling me to stop—you've got to teach me how to hit it harder!"

Because they can become so attached to doing these things, it does not usually help to just tell them to stop. They are probably not going to listen to you. **Rather than arguing with them, we want their own life experiences to inform them.** We want to very systematically go through everything they have ever tried to do to get rid of their anxiety, and ask them how it has worked for them. Only when they realize that it has not been working will they consider letting go of an old behavior. Eventually, clients come to realize that their attempts to control or avoid things, especially their own thoughts and feelings, are actually feeding their anxiety, not making it better.

I recently had a client, who I'll call Mary, with a lot of anxiety. In the first session, I told her it would be very important for us not to repeat past mistakes, and not to keep doing something if it didn't work. I told her I didn't want her to take my word for anything, but to let her own lived experience guide her. I asked her what she had already tried to do in her struggle with anxiety.

One of the first things that Mary said was "Well, I just try to tell myself I'm going to be okay, and that this is temporary, or I just try not to think about the things that worry me."

"Okay," I replied. "So, you try to use positive self-talk to talk yourself out of the anxious feelings, or you try to ignore the thoughts. How's that worked for you so far? How effective has it been?"

Her response was, "Well, sometimes it works maybe for a few days, but then I'll have another thought like 'Oh no, what if this anxiety causes a heart problem?!' Then that makes me anxious again."

"Okay, so it sounds like it works a little bit temporarily. But you also told me you have been struggling with this for years and years, so is it safe to say—and don't let me put words into your mouth—that talking yourself out of the thoughts or ignoring them has not been the ultimate solution to this problem? That it hasn't delivered the goods? That your life has not continued getting better just by fighting the thoughts?"

A small tear appeared in Mary's eye. "No, it only works temporarily at best. I just keep thinking that if I try harder and think more positively, it will work."

"So, maybe 'trying harder' is something we should add to the list. Has trying harder fixed everything?"

"No." More tears. "That's why I'm here."

Even if something does work, it may come with a cost. "So, thinking does help sometimes, which is why you have been doing it for so long. But do the temporary benefits come with any costs? Have there been any downsides to trying harder to think positive?"

Mary looked away. "Well, it has cost me a lot in my relationships, because I'm always thinking and worrying, and I'm not very present with my kids. In fact, I took my husband out for his birthday recently. Because our kids are so young, it was the first time in years that we had a date night for just the two of us. Then I had a thought that my heart doesn't feel right, and so I spent the whole dinner worrying about my heart. I kept crying, and my husband was frustrated, because he's so tired of me complaining all the time about my anxiety."

I said, "Okay, so these attempts to try to talk yourself out of the anxiety have also come with a price. Here's the thing, in our therapy sessions, we don't want to do more of something that you are telling me has not worked for you. If you've been using a proverbial hammer to deal with your anxious thoughts, you may think that I'm going to give you a sledgehammer to deal with them. And if that was working, I would help you do that. But based on your own experience, not what the textbooks might say or what other people have told you, it sounds like fighting these thoughts is just not working for you. So, can we agree not to fight the thoughts harder in here?"

Mary looked confused, which is one of the first signs of getting unstuck. "Well, if we don't fight the thoughts, what are we going to do then?"

"We'll explore that later on, but before we do anything, I think it is important that we not do the things that are not working for you so we don't waste our time in here. What else have you tried?"

She said, "Well, I've been on an SSRI medication."

"Okay," I replied. "How's that worked for you?"

"I felt like it took the edge off at first, but I feel some side effects, and I still get anxious all the time."

"Okay, so it sounds like it's helped you a little bit, but it's come with some side effects, and it's not been the solution." Now here's a hard question sometimes for therapists to ask. "What about therapy? Have you tried it before, and how was it for you?"

"Well, sometimes it helped to talk about my problems, and I would feel better during the sessions—"

"And yet you are back seeing another therapist," I interrupted. "Is it fair to say that the therapy you have done already has not worked for you? We need to make sure that we don't do here what you have done in the other therapies, because that hasn't been a solution for your struggle with anxiety. We're going to have to do something completely different here if you want things to be different in your life."

Very systematically, the therapist takes account of everything the client has tried so that the client feels motivated to stop doing what isn't working. In addition to helping them let go, this process is very empathic and validating of their lived experiences.

Tip for Clinicians ──────────────────────────────────────

Don't keep trying to talk clients out of what they are doing. This is likely to generate resistance and defensiveness. Be patient. After all, you know that what they are doing is not working, or they would not be in your office in the first place.

Use the next worksheet to help clients consider and let go of the things that have not been working in their attempts to control their anxiety.

Letting Go of What Doesn't Work

You have probably tried many different things in your attempts to get rid of your anxiety. While some of them may work a little, they probably have only been temporary solutions at best, or you would not be reading this right now.

Before we embark on a journey to live a more fulfilling life, we better be sure to not keep making the same mistakes that were made in the past. **Let's get really clear on what has not worked for you—we don't want to keep doing what doesn't work!** When you find yourself hitting your head against a brick wall, and the wall is not breaking, it's a bad idea to keep hitting your head harder and harder.

Here are some common things people do when they are struggling with anxiety, just to get you started:

- Thinking about your problems all day long
- Trying not to think about problems
- Delving into the past to try to figure out how this all got started
- Worrying about what's going to happen in the future
- Avoiding things, people, or situations that might make you anxious
- Fighting against or trying to talk yourself out of difficult thoughts and feelings
- Trying to think positive
- Blaming yourself or others
- Distracting yourself
- Taking medication
- Doing meditation
- Using drugs or alcohol
- Psychotherapy
- Reading self-help books
- Trying harder
- Giving up and doing nothing

As you go through this worksheet, it is important to be honest with yourself. Get in touch with your actual lived experience. It's easy to blame yourself or tell yourself that you didn't try hard enough (and you may need to add "trying harder" to your list of things that don't work). Maybe all the "experts" say what you tried "should" work. **But the bottom line is, did it work for you?**

Make copies of this worksheet, and fill it out for each thing you have already tried to do about your anxiety.

What have you already tried doing to deal with your anxiety?

_____

_____

_____

_____

How long have you been doing that? How has that worked for you? Did it supply a temporary or a permanent solution? Be honest with yourself. Let your own experience inform you.

_____

_____

_____

_____

What has that strategy cost you? What have been the negative "side effects" of using that strategy? What has that strategy caused you to give up?

_____

_____

_____

_____

In the service of living a more fulfilling life, are you willing to try something different? Are you willing to be flexible? Even if your mind tells you it doesn't want to? Even if you might feel uncomfortable feelings like anxiety? Even if you have good reasons to complain about all the awful things other people have done to you? In order to have a more fulfilling life, are you willing to try something new, even if you don't know what that something is yet?

_____

_____

_____

_____

Reflect on these questions with your therapist. It will help as you prepare to learn new ways of relating to anxious thoughts and feelings as you begin the journey to create a life worth living.

WILLINGNESS

Once clients have let go of what is not working, they need to be willing to do something new. Both letting go and doing new things are very scary for people, so it is important to foster a sense of willingness in our clients.

You can have brilliant intervention strategies for clients, but if they are not willing to do them, they are useless. If clients are not willing, the therapist has likely missed something. Perhaps the clients have lost touch with their values, or perhaps they are still clinging to the strategies that have not been working. In either case, it may be useful to go back to values exploration or creative hopelessness. We will also explore this further in the chapter on committed action.

I got my private pilot's license renewed a few years ago. In order to fly again, I had to be evaluated by and fly with a flight instructor. Even though I liked the flight instructor, just the thought of going through the whole process, especially with someone constantly judging me, created some anxiety. Would I remember how to communicate on the radio? Would I miss something on the checklists? What if I made an embarrassing bounce on the runway when I was landing the plane?

Even though the process made me anxious, I was willing to feel that anxiety and discomfort, because completing the checkride gave me the freedom to fly again. I just love taking my friends and family into the sky. Getting in touch with values creates a willingness to be uncomfortable.

Use the next handout to help clients connect to the importance of willingness.

Willingness

Can you remember a time when you accomplished something important, like graduating from school, getting married, or raising your kids? Did you have to do things that were uncomfortable? Did you have to do things you did not want to do? Why in the world would you have done those things if they came with suffering?

If you have a big enough reason to do something, you are willing to be uncomfortable. If you are a parent, I bet there is a long list of things you didn't want to do yet did for your child, like changing diapers, getting up in the middle of the night, or cleaning up vomit.

Would you want to run toward a poisonous snake? Probably not. What if your child or your best friend was about to step on one?

Would you be willing to stick your hands in feces if I asked you to? You wouldn't think so. But what if someone offered you one million dollars to do it? What if your child or friend fell into a giant pile of it and needed your help?

Now, the big question: **Are you willing to have uncomfortable thoughts and feelings like anxiety if it means you get to do more of the things that make life worth living?** Are you willing to let go of the old things you've been doing that are no longer working for you? Are you willing to try something new? Are you willing to not know what's next?

After all, if your thinking mind could fix this anxiety, you would not still be struggling. Therefore, you cannot know in words how you will proceed.

I'm certainly not asking you to wallow in your suffering. Your therapist can teach you new ways of relating to the ruminations, worries, and anxiety. But if you keep doing what you've always done, you will keep getting what you've always gotten. How long have you suffered? Are you ready to let go of what you've been doing and do something different?

On a scale of 1-10, how willing are you to do something different? _____

If you wrote a number that is less than 10, what would it take to raise that willingness one or two more points? What is getting in the way of being fully willing?

Consider your reasons for working through your struggles with anxiety. Hasn't it been easier sometimes to try to run away from it? But what has that cost you? Think about the things in your life that really matter, the things that light you up. They may be hard to bring to mind when your life has been about just surviving with this anxiety for so long, just getting through your day. **Take some time to get in touch with what would**

really make your life worth living. Can you find something important enough to be more willing to be courageous and try something different?

Don't worry about how to get there just yet. You and your therapist can work together to create a plan, and you can experiment to find out what works best for your own life. However, the best plans are useless if you are not willing to do something different.

Chapter 4

You Are Not Your Anxiety: Expanding Your Sense of Self

Clients often have such intense anxiety that their sense of identity becomes fused with their anxious feelings and thoughts. The words in their head become conditioned to automatically feel anxiety, which sparks more anxious thinking, and their sense of self becomes narrow. This chapter will provide exercises and worksheets to give clients a bigger sense of who they really are. Recognizing that you are much more than any of the problems you have enables you to gain a broader perspective on things and engage in a more meaningful life.

ATTACHMENT TO A CONCEPTUALIZED SELF

When you rigidly hold on to a fixed idea of who you are, you become inflexible (Hayes, 2007). Think about the clients you have had that have gotten really stuck in their problems. Too often, **their problems become their identities**.

Twelve-step programs, like Alcoholics Anonymous, have literally changed millions of lives, and they have greatly benefited many of my own clients. However, I have sometimes noticed an interesting phenomenon. Some of the people in these programs begin to overly identify themselves as just an alcoholic or an addict, as if that is all they are. Now of course, they need to pay attention to that aspect of who they are, especially if they have been in denial, but sometimes their entire lives become all about not using. When your identity is about not doing something, you end up thinking about it all the time, rather than moving toward your values. In my experience, most of the clients who overcome their challenges with addictions pay attention to that aspect of themselves, but they also identify with a bigger sense of who they are, like their identity as a parent, a partner, a spiritual person, and/or a worker. When you are more than just your addiction, you will be more flexible to do the things that lead to a meaningful life.

When I was younger, I owned a martial arts school. My ninja teacher, Stephen K. Hayes, appreciated history and tradition, but he would say that the most traditional thing we can do is to be modern. In other words, when the "traditional" techniques were developed, they were considered cutting edge. We don't have to do things exactly as they did 800 years ago. The important thing is to understand the principles and apply them in a modern context.

After decades of studying education theory and pedagogy, our teacher decided to revamp the training curriculum for our martial art. When he brought all of the instructors together from around the world to share the new curriculum, people literally rebelled, because their entire identities were caught up in how they ran their schools. "No! I don't want to change what I'm doing! I want to keep doing it the traditional way!" Our teacher replied, "Well, what you are calling the 'traditional way' is something

I made up decades ago. Now I've found a much better way to teach these principles for modern self-defense."

Personally, I didn't get caught up in the rebellion, because my entire identity was not tied into being a martial arts school owner. I had a family, career, hobbies, and other roles and interests, so I was much more flexible about how to run my school. My attitude was, "Okay, if you think this is going to help more people, let's go for it." The people who saw only one way to run their schools were unable to adapt. Their schools ended up staying very small, and many even closed down, because they couldn't be flexible.

Likewise, clients with anxiety often say, "I'm an anxious person." **When anxiety becomes your identity, it is hard to be flexible.** After all, anxious people tend not to go out and have fun, give public talks, take risks, or make efforts to create rich, meaningful lives.

SELF AS CONTEXT

In ACT, the tendency to identify oneself with the **content** of one's thoughts, feelings, experiences, and roles is referred to as "self as content" (Foody, Barnes-Holmes, & Barnes-Holmes, 2012; Hayes, Strosahl, & Wilson, 2012). It is hard to be flexible if you think you *are* your anxious thoughts and feelings.

However, we can help clients realize that they are so much more than just their thoughts, their problems, and their anxiety. Shifting to "self as context" involves recognizing that who you are is the **context** in which you *have* thoughts, you *have* feelings, and you *have* sensations. If you can have any of those experiences, you must be bigger than them.

This is not just a trick for getting rid of anxiety. It's about helping clients **make room for these thoughts, emotions, and sensations.** You learn to have compassion for yourself, for your own thoughts and experiences, instead of fighting with them and struggling with them. This is a very different approach—when people are fighting anxious thoughts and feelings, they are only fighting themselves. No wonder they can struggle for a lifetime. They seem to sometimes win battles with themselves, but they can never win a war against themselves.

Tip for Clinicians ————————————————————————————————

Remember to practice getting in touch with a bigger sense of who you are. If you are too caught up in your identity as a clinician, you will become inflexible. Remember that your clinical work is only one part of who you are. You are so much more, so practice reconnecting to all of the other aspects of yourself.

Interestingly, clients will sometimes ask, "Well gee—if I'm not my thoughts, then who am I?" This is quite a profound question! Philosophers and theologians have debated this question for thousands of years. Some people might get into spiritual interpretations about the soul. Others take a scientific approach that we are ever-changing conglomerations of different processes of which there is no one unchanging essence (Sears, 2017b). But when this comes up in therapy, I usually just say, "Well, that's a great question, but for our work here in therapy, it is important to realize that you are more than the thoughts, emotions, or experiences you are having. Some call the process the 'observer self,' that part of you that notices your own experiences and is aware of your own history."

Use the following worksheet to help clients explore their ideas about who they are.

Who Am I?

Life can sometimes seem very overwhelming. While we all have very real problems in our lives, too often, **we get so lost in our problems and our anxieties that we forget who we really are**. The following worksheet can help you get back in touch with the fact that you are so much more than what you are dealing with right now.

Sit in a quiet place and allow your mind to settle as best you can. Repeat to yourself the questions, "Who am I?" and "What am I?" and see what comes to mind. To get you started, some categories that your answers might fit into are listed below, but you do not have to limit your answers to these areas. Just see what comes up in your mind when you sit with those questions.

Names and nicknames I have gone by:

_____

_____

_____

Jobs I have held:

_____

_____

_____

Relationship roles I have had (father, mother, son, daughter, worker, etc.):

_____

_____

_____

Things I have been called:

_____

_____

_____

Things I have called myself:

_____

_____

_____

Physical descriptions of who I am:

_____

_____

_____

Problems I have had:

_____

_____

_____

Successes I have enjoyed:

_____

_____

_____

Other answers to the questions "Who am I?" and "What am I?":

_____

_____

_____

_____

_____

As you do this exercise, and perhaps repeat it several times, you will begin to see that who you are is much more than what you are able to perceive in any one moment. While your problems may not go away, they can seem less overwhelming when you remember that your problems don't have to define you.

THE CHESSBOARD METAPHOR

It can be very challenging for clients to understand the difference between self as content and self as context. Since their so-called good thoughts and bad thoughts often seem to be stuck in a life-and-death battle, many clients appreciate the chessboard metaphor (Bach & Moran, 2008; Hayes, Strosahl, & Wilson, 2012). Note, as with all of the ACT processes, this is not just about self as context, but also touches on the other six processes, such as defusion. The point is to help clients realize that they are so much more than the battling pieces in their minds.

As with the other handouts, therapists can walk clients through this, and/or give the handout to clients to read and consider at home between sessions.

The Chess Game in Your Head

When you struggle with anxiety, your mind is often full of anxious thoughts. These thoughts can seem to get mixed up with your entire sense of identity. But as strange as it might sound, **you are not really who you *think* you are**, because you are more than just thoughts.

I was once working with a woman named Mary who could not stop thinking anxious thoughts. "What if I get sick? What if the stock market crashes and we lose our retirement? What if my partner stops loving me? What if things get worse at work? What if something happens to my kids? What if I crack under all this pressure? Why can't I stop worrying? What's wrong with me?"

Right after these kinds of thoughts, another part of her brain would say, "Oh come on, I can't control whether or not I'll get sick. We've got a financial plan, so we'll recover eventually from a market crash. I know my partner really loves me. Work is not that bad. My kids will be fine. I can handle things. I'm a strong person."

But then, more anxious thoughts would pop up. "But if I did get really sick, how could I manage things? What if all our money is lost just before retirement? What if my partner gets tired of me because I worry all the time? What if our company gets bought out and my new boss is rude to me? What if my kids get hurt really badly on the playground? I just can't pull myself together!"

As Mary described how her thoughts kept going back and forth, I said, "Wow, it sounds like there's a chess match going on in your head right now. The anxious thoughts are telling you things are going to be bad, then positive thoughts tell you that things are going to be okay, then more anxious thoughts, then more positive thoughts. All day long, the 'good' and 'bad' thoughts just keep going back and forth, back and forth. If we view this as a chess match, and the 'good' thoughts are one side, and the 'bad' thoughts are the other side, what would you identify as you?"

Mary paused for a moment, and said, "Well, I guess I'm the good side, the side that is giving the positive thoughts, and saying everything is going to be okay."

With a twinkle in my eye, I asked, "Then where are all the other thoughts coming from?"

After a longer pause, Mary said, "I guess I'm those thoughts too."

I leaned forward. "See if you can take a bigger-picture look at all this stuff. If this is a big chess game, where is the 'you' in all of the battling that is going on back and forth?"

After sitting in silence for about a minute, Mary become tearful. She looked up and said, "Hmm—I must be the chess board!"

When you are having anxious thoughts, they can seem so strong and powerful. If you think these thoughts are who you are, if you take yourself to be the *content* of the thoughts, it is like identifying with the pieces on a chessboard. If you are the pieces, let's say the black side, then you have got to win against the white side. You feel very strongly that you must move to take out the white pieces, and you try hard to avoid losing your own pieces. You work hard to develop strategies to fight the other pieces, and you get upset if you lose a piece. You get really caught up in the drama.

But can you see, who you are is the *context* in which this battle is going on. You are much more like the chessboard. There could not even be a chess game without the chessboard. There would be no anxiety, no thoughts, no experiences, and no problems without *you*. **You are the bigger context in which all of these things come and go.**

In this metaphor, the chessboard doesn't even care which side wins or loses. It's not caught up in the drama. It's not scarred by the battle. Likewise, you can practice stepping back from the battles going on inside of you, and simply notice, "Ah, here I go arguing with myself again about what I should have done in the past. There I go again, telling myself I'm not a good person. My old friend anxiety is showing up. My heart is beating quickly, and my stomach is churning." You can remind yourself that those thoughts and feelings are not who you are. They are just things happening in your mind and body right now. Who you are is so much more.

Importantly, **you don't have to like the thoughts or feel good about the anxiety**. The point is that you are more than those things. When you remember that, you become more flexible to do what really matters in your life. After all, when you are fighting with your thoughts and feelings, you are probably not attending to what is most important, like spending time with family or engaging in the activities that make your life truly worth living.

Of course, you can still play the chess game whenever you want. You can even lose yourself in the game if you like. However, it can be very helpful to keep in the back of your mind that *you* are not the game.

THE SENSE OF SELF ACROSS A LIFETIME

Another way to expand the sense of self is to recognize that there is so much more to us than what we are experiencing now. We can recognize that we have literally been many different selves across our lifetimes. Who we are now is very different than who we were as a toddler, a grade-schooler, a high schooler, or as a young adult. And yet, there is a thread which connects all of these very different "selves."

The picture above represents just a few of the many selves I have experienced. These are only a few snapshots of moments in my life when I was very different than I am in this moment: playing "biddy ball" in grade school, doing ninja training as a teenager, visiting temples in India and Nepal, receiving transmission as a Zen master, and thrusting a spear into an attacker when I was teaching a workshop. We have many different aspects of who we are, and yet there is a sort of cohesion, a thread that connects all of our experiences throughout this lifetime.

The following exercise is designed to help clients break out of the narrow viewpoint of the anxious self they may believe themselves to currently be. You can read this exercise to a client as a script during a therapy session, and/or you can give the handout as homework.

Tip for Clinicians

When leading exercises for a group of clients, experience will help you find a balance between being too vague or too specific. If you are too vague when you lead an exercise, clients feel confused and have a hard time getting into it. On the other hand, if you get too specific, you may only be sharing what works for you, and you may close off the client's ability to creatively adapt the exercise to what works best for them. If you are leading an exercise in individual therapy, you can have the person talk to you while they are doing it, if they're comfortable doing so, allowing you to customize the experience for each client.

Expanding Your Sense of Self

Our problems and our anxieties can become so big that they become our whole lives, and even our entire identity. Practice the exercise below to put this moment in time and your anxieties into a bigger context, and **to get more in touch with a bigger sense of who you really are**.

Find a quiet, comfortable place to sit, ideally where you won't be interrupted for a few minutes. You can experiment with doing this exercise with your eyes closed or slightly open.

See if you can set aside all the things you need to think about later. You may be used to being very busy, and your mind may automatically want to bring up your to-do lists. Just give yourself permission to be here for yourself for a few moments. Everything will still be there later.

To begin, see if you can bring up some very early memories of when you were a toddler or a preschooler. The point of this is not to bring up traumatic memories, so if you notice traumatic memories coming up, you can just set them aside. The main thing to remember is what it felt like to be *you* in a preschooler body. Can you remember that? Your little body looked totally different than it did after you grew up. You probably had to look up at doorknobs and counters. You definitely had to look up at all the adults. Your hand felt really small when an adult held your hand.

Chances are you had different thoughts, different beliefs, and different feelings than you did after you grew up. Certain things mattered to you, certain things worried you, and certain things made you happy.

As you do this, some specific memories might come to mind. Or, you might remember being in a specific house, daycare, or a park. Or you might have only a vague sense of your surroundings. The main thing is to take a couple of minutes to remember what it felt like to be *you* when you were somewhere around preschool age.

If strong feelings or thoughts do come up at any time during this exercise, you don't have to change them or fix them right now. Just notice them as they are, as best you can, and move on with the exercise. You can always bring them up later with your therapist if you so choose. For now, just get in touch with the part of you that observed your experiences.

Next, fast forward a little to grade-school age. The exact age is not important—just see if you can bring to mind what it was like to be *you* when you were in grade school. Remember what your body looked like, the way you thought, and some of the ways you felt. Again, you might have just a general sense, or you may have a specific memory, maybe of being in a house, an apartment, a school, or at a playground. See if you can remember how it felt to look out from those young eyes, what it felt like to be the *you* that noticed the things around you. Spend a few minutes bringing up what it felt like to be you in that small, grade-school aged body.

Now, fast forward to a time when you were in high school. Just see if you can remember what it felt like to be *you* at that age. What was it like to look out from those eyes, to feel the things you felt, and to have the thoughts that you had back then? As a teenager, you probably had a lot of problems, or at least some problems, that seemed so important to you at that time in your life. Maybe you had some wonderful experiences. No need to necessarily dwell on any specific problem or joy. Just spend a couple of minutes getting in touch with what it felt like to be *you* as a teenager.

For the next few minutes, fast forward to a time when you were a young adult. (If you consider yourself a young adult now, just think back a year or two ago.) Again, remember what it felt like to be *you* when you were that young adult. Bring up some of the thoughts and beliefs you had. You likely had problems that you were dealing with at different times, maybe things you were passionate about, and certain worries or concerns. You might bring to mind being in school, or working a job, or you can just bring up a more general sense of being that age. Spend a few minutes remembering what it felt like to be *you* as a young adult.

Now, bring your attention into this present moment. With your eyes still closed, or slightly open, just see if you can become more aware of the *you* that you feel yourself to be right now. There is a *you* that is here in this moment, observing your experiences. A *you* that is feeling the surface you are sitting or standing on, feeling the clothing on your skin, and feeling your belly moving as you breathe. There is a *you* that is aware of the sounds going on around you. A *you* that is aware of any thoughts or feelings that are here right now. Spend a few moments getting in touch with this bigger sense of who you are, with this *you* that is experiencing the experiences, and is noticing what you are noticing.

And now, reflect back through all those times, and all those *yous* that you just remembered. Who you are now is much different than the *you* that you were as a preschooler, grade schooler, high schooler, or young adult. And yet, there is a sort of thread that connects, at least through your memory, all those different times. Even though you have changed in a lot of ways, there is still a thread that is you. There is a *you* that has had this history. This *you* has had all kinds of thoughts, feelings, opinions, joys, and problems, and those have changed a lot over the years. Here you are in this moment, with your thoughts, feelings, anxieties, and problems.

See if you can experience this *you* in a bigger context, a *you* that is observing just one moment in the many moments that make up your life. See if you can get in touch with that bigger sense of who you are, beyond what you might be dealing with in this moment. There is a *you* that can notice these problems, and can have thoughts, feelings, sensations, and sense experiences. Some call this the "observer self." It is the bigger sense of *you* that is noticing all these different times in your life, and noticing what you are experiencing right now. This certainly doesn't mean your problems are not important. For now, just spend a few moments getting in touch with that bigger sense of who you are.

Before ending this exercise, remember that **this bigger sense of self is something you can always access**. It is always there, noticing what is going on. It only gets lost when we get caught up in thoughts, feelings, and problems, and forget who we really are.

Now let this exercise go. Slowly bring your attention back to the rest of the room, and allow your eyes to come fully open.

Jot down a few notes about what you experienced. Repeat this exercise a number of times, and see if you notice any patterns, or if any new insights occur to you.

PROCESSING THE EXERCISE

If you walk a client through the previous exercise, it can be helpful to process what they experience. While the main point is to help clients expand their sense of self, and to see themselves as more than the distressing thoughts, feelings, and problems they may have now, they often have other interesting experiences.

Sometimes after doing this exercise, people come to realize that the things that seemed so awful at the time were not really a big deal when they look back on it. They often come to see their life challenges in a bigger context. I once knew a person who had a little cartoon on her wall that said, "Wake-up call number 147: Nobody really cares that you had a 4.0 GPA in high school." In the context of her entire life, it wasn't that important. She realized that she had experienced so much anxiety and gave up so many leisure activities to get perfect scores. Every now and then, she still has nightmares that she is taking a test but was unable to study for it. Funny how those old thoughts and feelings can become such a part of our identities.

Now, those memories might still pop up automatically, but you can learn to be kind to yourself when they do arise. You can learn to just notice those old feelings, and you can begin to recognize that you are so much more than that now. We don't erase our histories, we just get less caught up in them, less rigidly defined by them.

After doing this exercise, some clients notice certain patterns of values that have been consistent throughout their lives. They can sometimes even forget that there were things that made them happy in the past, or they may realize that they had lost touch with important aspects of their identities that had been closed off for years.

After doing this exercise, I once had a client say, "You know, I was remembering childhood, and it was pretty happy. Then we got to the high school years, and it was really tumultuous. Coming into now, I'm realizing that a big part of my identity is either related to, or a reaction to, my high school self, which is an interesting thing. I've sort of over-identified myself with who I was in high school. I've been forgetting that I am much more than that. Even me trying not to be that high schooler anymore is still kind of being hooked into that, if that makes any sense." That made perfect sense to me—you're not really free to be yourself if you are still rebelling against other identities.

Clients sometimes think of themselves as always having been "broken." Through this exercise, they may come to realize that they have had many other experiences over the course of their lifetime. They may have forgotten some of their happier memories.

Sometimes people with a history of trauma experience interesting things during this exercise. I once worked with a woman who went through terrible childhood abuse. After her parents passed away, her siblings found a box of old pictures. They said they didn't want them and gave them to her. Her dad had been an amateur photographer and had a large collection of photographs. As she looked through these old pictures, she found quite a few of herself when she was a child, and she noticed that she was smiling in some of them. She had found a lot of photos of times she and her father would set up the camera outside during lightning storms. Since this was before the age of digital photography, she and her father had to be very patient to capture lightning flashes. She began to remember that she had a lot of fun on those evenings with her father. Those positive feelings of being with her abusive father made her question herself. She even began to wonder if she had made up her traumatic memories and wondered if maybe her childhood had not been as bad as she thought it had been.

In her mind, she was an abuse survivor. It had become her entire identity. It took her some time to integrate the fact that she could have been abused, and that she could have had good memories sometimes as well. Just because you had some happy memories doesn't take away the awfulness of the abuse. Her abuse was very real and was a big part of who she ended up becoming, but it wasn't the whole of her experience. Clients can get really confused when they start to recognize that they are more than just the bad things that happened to them, but it is an important step to becoming more flexible.

Since this exercise is about expanding the sense of self, the script suggests setting aside any traumatic memories that come up. However, if such memories do arise in a therapy session, I may or may not explore them. The important thing is to model that these memories are not experiences that we have to automatically struggle with or run away from. One option is to say, "Okay, so you're noticing that memory is coming up. Can you get in touch with the 'you' that went through that experience?" You could take it in a lot of different directions, depending on how well you know the client, how long you have been working together, and how good your rapport is. You might simply say, "Let's just sit with that for a while." Then you might suggest, "Can you think of other times when you were that age?" The therapist's attitude is important, because we can accidently foster avoidance by saying, "Well, we can't think about that. Let's get away from it." It tends to be better to calmly say, "Well, just notice if something traumatic does come up, and let's just look for some other memories right now."

MOVING TO A UNIVERSAL CONTEXT

As we've been discussing, when your clients are just their problems or their anxiety, their lives tend to not be very fulfilling. They lose touch with their values, with a bigger sense of what life is all about.

While not every client will be ready or even interested in this, we can give clients the ultimate context of who they are by expanding to a universal sense of self. Many clients may define this through their religion or through their personal sense of spirituality. However, I find that even taking a purely practical, scientific approach can help shift clients away from their narrow views of who they really are and can put their problems and anxieties in context.

As with the other exercises in this workbook, you can read the next handout to clients as a script and/ or give it to them to practice as homework. If you find this one interesting, there is a book full of such ponderings in *The Sense of Self* (Sears, 2017b). I also highly recommend the works of Alan Watts (e.g., Watts, 2004).

Cosmic Self Meditation

For human beings, having problems is part of life, and sometimes these problems seem overwhelming. But because our wonderfully evolved brains have the ability to reflect on the past and plan for the future, we also can get caught up in anxiously worrying about what was and what might be. Through our thinking and through societal programming, **we can completely identify with our problems and worries and forget who we really are**.

To reconnect with the bigger context of who you are and where you come from, you can meditate on the sentences below. Find a quiet, peaceful place to sit. Ideally, read through this meditative practice in nature, or you can pause to close your eyes from time to time to consider these words.

This exercise is a meditation to contemplate how who you are is really interdependent with the environment and, indeed, the entire universe. We tend to feel like isolated beings, so different and separate from everything around us.

Imagine for a moment that you are a leaf on a tree. If you believe that you are only that leaf, you will be sad when you wither and fall off the branch. But the leaf cannot exist without the entire tree. It was never separate from it. It grew out of it. After it falls to the ground, it will be reabsorbed by the tree, and new leaves will grow.

Likewise, how can you be a separate human being? Your skin is not a boundary that separates you from the world. It joins you to your surroundings. It is a way of connecting with the air, the sunshine, and the earth. You could not possibly exist in isolation. You are dependent on a combination of countless things to be alive. The food you eat flows through you and is all produced by the Earth. You need all these things in your environment just as much as you need a heart and lungs. And it took the entire Earth to create this environment.

Where else could you come from if not from this Earth? **You are not a stranger that was thrust into this world. You literally grew out of the Earth.** And the Earth can only exist because of a sun, which moves through the Milky Way galaxy, which formed out of the universe.

The universe appears to have exploded out of nothingness. Hydrogen atoms came together to form stars, which crushed the atoms into denser elements, which later exploded out into space. These atoms eventually came together to form solar systems. At least on planet Earth, these elements developed into self-replicating life forms. Over billions of years, human beings came about. Your ancestors produced your parents, and they produced you.

Your physical being is literally billions of years old, made of the very material that first exploded out into the universe after the Big Bang. The physical being you identify with may come and go, but it does not disappear—it merely changes form. Just as a leaf develops and then transforms back into new leaves, your atoms came together from the environment, and will transform back into new life, and new babies.

You might also imagine the universe as the ocean. If you identify yourself with one of the waves, you may get caught up in competing with the other waves, or you might try to hold on and preserve the wave. But waves are only moving water, and you cannot hold onto them. The waves of the ocean come and go, but they are all forms created by the entire ocean. Likewise, you are a physical manifestation that was created by countless processes throughout the universe. The universe is waving "you."

At first, these thoughts may feel depressing. You may feel that you are losing yourself, like a drop of water disappearing into a vast ocean. But the opposite is actually true. You are not the drop, you are the entire ocean. You can enjoy the wave all the more, even with its transience, knowing that you are more than just the wave.

The entire universe is playing the role of you and is doing such a convincing job of it that even you have been fooled. You have simply forgotten that you are so much more than an isolated bag of skin. You are the entire universe experiencing itself through a particular point of view.

Just reading through this meditation the first few times may only feel like an intellectual exercise, but we tend to become what we program our minds to be. If you only think about problems and struggling for survival, your mind will be programmed to be anxious. Over time, the feeling that you are more than just an isolated individual will begin to sink in and feel like common sense.

Of course, you will still need to earn a living, pay your bills, engage in your relationships, and deal with your problems. But if you practice this exercise on a regular basis, the things in your life that bother you so much right now may just create a little less anxiety. When you remember the big picture of who you really are, you can still play the game, but you get less caught up in it.

Tip for Clinicians ──────────────────────────────────

Remember that our clients, no matter how much they are struggling, are human beings. Sometimes clinicians contribute to clients' constricted sense of self by labeling them by their diagnoses. While helping them with their presenting issues is important, do not forget that they are so much more than that. Help them to remember that too. A client with anxiety may also be a parent, a child, a cousin, a dreamer, a lover, a helper, a yoga practitioner, a science geek, and a human being who craves connection, among thousands of other things.

The good news is that even if your clients never quite understand intellectually that they are more than their problems and their anxiety, if you as the therapist relate to them from this broader vantage point, it can help them become more flexible.

While fixed ideas about the self create inflexibility, attachment to thoughts in general also contribute to inflexibility. In the next chapter, we will explore the principle of defusion, which involves relating differently to thoughts.

Chapter 5

Defusion: Letting Go of the Battle with Anxious Thinking

Clients with anxiety often get caught up in negative thinking patterns, spending countless hours battling with their own thoughts. The most positive thoughts don't change the anxiety in the long term, because they find loopholes in even the most logical counterarguments. Even when they know they are untrue, they just can't seem to stop the distressing thoughts. Old messages from their past often tell them that they will never change, or that they do not deserve a better life. Habits of thinking keep them worried about scary future possibilities. This chapter will provide exercises and worksheets to help clients develop a new relationship to their thoughts so that they can rise above the traps created by the thinking process and move toward what matters to them.

COGNITIVE FUSION: CONFUSING THOUGHTS WITH REALITY

Cognitive fusion refers to the tendency human beings have to become fused, or attached, to their thinking (Blackledge, 2007; Hayes, Strosahl, & Wilson, 2012). Clients with anxiety have a strong tendency to become stuck in certain thinking patterns, and **these thoughts become fused with strongly conditioned emotions, memories, and associations**. I'll bet you can think of quite a few clients who were very fixated on a certain way of thinking, and you simply could not talk them out of it, even though on the surface the thoughts seemed ridiculous.

I once had a client with health anxiety who would come in with a different distressing thought almost every week. One week, she said, "Somebody told me I should look into bipolar, so I looked it up on the internet. Now I am terrified that I have bipolar disorder!"

I had been working with this client for years. I've worked on acute inpatient psychiatric units, and I have had a lot of clients with bipolar disorder. I know bipolar. She is not bipolar. She has anxiety. In fact, I told her that her obsession with wondering whether or not she has bipolar is a symptom of anxiety. In the session, I even got out the DSM-5® and we walked through the diagnostic criteria for bipolar disorder. I explained the difference between hypomania, mania, and anxiety very thoroughly, and she felt relieved by the end of the session. Then, later that night, she left a voicemail message saying, "Please tell me again that I don't have bipolar disorder!"

The client had become fused with that thought. In the next session, we worked on relating differently to it. "Okay, so you're noticing the thought that you have bipolar. That's it. It is just a thought in your head. You don't have to argue with it. It's not like there is an actual psychiatrist in your head saying, 'Well, you need to convince me that your symptoms are other than what they appear to me.' These thoughts are literally just sounds inside your head, so you can practice simply noticing, 'Oh, there's that thought again. The voice of anxiety is echoing in my head.'"

This is a very different approach to working with thoughts. When clients don't believe you, and keep wanting you to argue with their thoughts, you can simply ask, "Okay, how has fighting with these thoughts been working for you?" They will likely say, "Well, it doesn't work for very long." To which you can reply, "Then why do want me to keep fighting these thoughts?"

Certainly, it is important to have good rapport with clients, and be careful not to make it sound like you are making fun of them. But arguing with clients usually doesn't help. When this woman came into yet another session and again said, "Just tell me again I don't have bipolar," I replied, "I already told you that a number of times, but the thought keeps coming back anyway. This thought is very sticky for you, and it looks like arguing with that thought isn't working. It strikes me that the real problem is that you are anxious, so let's look at the anxiety, and then you won't have to worry about whether or not you have bipolar disorder."

Tip for Clinicians ──

Don't get caught up in arguments about whether a client's thoughts are true or not. Help them examine the function of that thinking. "Is your thinking giving you a richer life?" "Are these thoughts enriching your relationships?" "I really don't know if your thoughts are right or wrong, but it sounds like this way of thinking is not working for you. It's not a good idea to keep doing something that doesn't work. Are you willing to do something different with these thoughts?"

THE PROBLEM WITH TRYING TO STOP THOUGHTS

There is an old technique called "thought stopping," in which you basically tell yourself to "stop it" when a thought comes up that you don't want. While doing this can sometimes have value as a way of disrupting automatic patterns, its effects tend to be temporary at best.

In fact, it is important for clients to realize that we cannot force our brains to stop thinking. I tell clients that this may sound like bad news at first, but it turns out to be good news, because it validates their own experiences. **Thoughts can literally be classically conditioned to come up, so fighting with them only gives them more emotional power.**

The following handout explains this concept to clients.

The Futility of Trying to Stop
Unwanted Thoughts

Imagine if I were to say to you, "Please, don't think of a pink elephant, or the ceiling is going to collapse! If you think of a pink elephant, you're going to die! So please, don't think about a pink elephant!" Your brain will end up thinking about what it is not supposed to think about. **You can't permanently stop thoughts even when your life depends on it!**

The good news is that we can learn to accept that this is simply what brains do. **We can learn to relate to our automatic thoughts differently.** Instead of getting stuck in trying to stop unwanted thoughts, we can have an attitude of, "Look there, my mind is at it again."

I know what you are going to think 10 seconds from now. Do you believe that? I know what you are going to think in five seconds, but you don't even know yourself. Mary had a little…

When I am giving live presentations, people often say "lamb" out loud. They cannot help themselves. Of course, if you did not hear this when you were growing up, you have no idea what I'm talking about. Mary could have anything—maybe an anaconda? This shows how arbitrary our automatic thoughts can be.

If you grew up hearing, "Mary had a little lamb," you can't help saying or thinking "lamb" when you hear, "Mary had a little…" Your brain has been programmed to say lamb automatically.

Every now and then someone tells me, "Well I didn't think lamb!" They don't realize that they just did!

The fact is, you just can't always stop your thoughts. If I were to tell you right now, "Don't think lamb! Lamb is a bad word! If you think lamb, you are a bad person!"

Mary had a little…

Your brain can't help it. You might be able to suppress it for a little while, or you might be able to distract yourself for a little while. But even with a lot of effort, it will keep popping out. It's just what your brain is going to do. It is futile to get caught up in trying to stop your thoughts or to "fix" them.

While that may be a pretty benign example, our brain does this all the time with a wide variety of thoughts, especially anxious ones. A person may have a thought "When I'm in a relationship…," and without being able to help it, they automatically add, "they are going to cheat on me." Now it is quite possible that in the past that was true, so the person learned to have that thought. Perhaps to be spared from heartbreak, the person learned, "I'm going to be cheated on, so don't be naive."

If someone doesn't realize that thought is going on automatically, they may not question it. They may become paranoid in their relationships, and ironically, push their partner away because of their mistrust. Or, they end up fighting with the thought. "Don't think that! Stop it! Why do I keep thinking that?"

It can be helpful to realize that **this is just what the brain does**. There is no need to try to stop the thoughts, because you can't anyway. The effort just causes more frustration and more thoughts. You don't have to talk back to your own thoughts. You don't have to buy into them. You don't have to argue with them. You don't have to like the thoughts, but you can learn to just let them flow through your head.

We learn things so easily, and our brains are doing this all the time automatically. Sometimes this learning is helpful, and sometimes it is not, but you are just not going to be able to control your thoughts with more thoughts.

Steve Hayes (2007) gives an example to show how easy it is to program the mind. While I don't have this kind of money, imagine if I were to tell you that I'm going to give you a million dollars the next time I see you if you can simply remember three numbers. The numbers are 7, 8, 9. Do you think you could remember those numbers five minutes from now? An hour from now? Tomorrow?

Do you think maybe a month from now, if I met you in person, and you told me you read this book, and I asked you what the numbers were, that you might be able to remember them? If you don't think so, you could practice a few more times.

Is it possible that a few years from now, if I asked you, "What are my numbers?," that you would be able to say 7, 8, 9? Now I wouldn't do this to you, but do think it's even possible that if I approached you on your death bed, and I asked you, "What are my numbers?," that you might just be able to remember, 7, 8, 9?

Whether or not you ever get a million dollars, those numbers were just programmed into your brain. If that silly little example can do that, just imagine all the times you have heard things like "You're stupid!," "You're weak for not controlling your anxiety!," "You're no good!," "You'll never amount to anything!," or "What's wrong with you?!"

Interestingly, research suggests that you never really unlearn anything. What you can do is override previous learning, or reduce the importance of previous learning, but the connections are still somewhere down there inside your brain. In other words, old automatic thoughts can come up seemingly out of nowhere. Have you ever found yourself accidentally saying something one of your parents said, even though you told yourself when you were younger that you would never ever say that in your life? It's just old stuff that got put in your head. **The good news is that just because it pops up doesn't mean you have to buy into it, get stuck in it, or act on it.**

Our anxious thoughts can easily get wired with emotions, which is why they seem so strong. This is also why fighting with them makes the thoughts stronger: You are simply adding more emotion to them. It seems ironic, but when you let go of trying to stop the thoughts, you will create a space in which you can relate to them differently.

THOUGHTS ARE JUST SOUNDS IN YOUR HEAD

As described in chapter 1, RFT (Torneke, Barnes-Holmes, & Hayes, 2010) is an important foundation of ACT, and helps us relate to thoughts differently than most of us have been taught in graduate school. It also seems to contradict the so-called common-sense view of thinking that most of us internalize when we are growing up.

RFT shows us that **words only have the meaning or power that our brains attach to them.** RFT describes how the human brain creates frames of relationships. The brain hears a sound (a word), and it conditions that sound with a certain meaning, association, or emotion. According to classical learning theory, you should only be able to make the connections that you actually experience. If I were to say to you "Watch out for that tiger!," according to traditional learning theory, you shouldn't feel scared unless you've actually experienced seeing a tiger while somebody says, "Watch out for that tiger!"

In actuality, when you are young, you learn how to say and later spell the word "tiger." The word gets associated with pictures of tigers, or perhaps cute little stuffed tigers, and you might feel warm and fuzzy when you hear the word "tiger." When you get older, you might see a National Geographic video of a tiger eating an antelope, and your brain connects the word tiger with what you witnessed in that video. If then I say, "Watch out for that tiger," you will feel scared, because your brain has created a frame of "tiger" and something getting eaten, which could mean that you could get eaten. RFT is quite a sophisticated theory, but it basically shows that your brain can create internal connections with thoughts and emotions without actually experiencing the events. While this might be useful in the case of actually encountering a wild tiger, other thoughts can get conditioned with anxiety in less useful ways. Thoughts, which are internal representations, can become conditioned with anxiety, such that **even having a thought, without a physical reality present, can produce intense anxiety.**

We forget that thoughts are just words, and words are just sounds. Take the word "water." If I ask someone, "Could you please give me a bottle of water?" and they hand it to me, I get reinforced by actually getting to drink the water and quench my thirst. **This is the good thing about conditioning words with meanings.**

This may sound obvious, but we can get into trouble when we forget that the clear liquid substance that I drink is not "water." "Water" is the sound that refers to that liquid reality. A cold liquid splashing your face or going down your throat is different from the sound "water." It's an experience. It's a phenomenon. It's different than the sound that represents it. Words are useful to have as representations, but we often forget that they are representations. **We get caught up in the representations as if they are real, like confusing a map with the territory it represents.**

Though it can be done with literally any word or sentence, one of the ways to help clients get a sense of what we are discussing above is through the "lemon exercise" (Hayes, Strosahl, & Wilson, 2012; Moran, 2011). I want you to imagine right now that there is a big, juicy lemon in front of you. Imagine you pick up a knife and cut that lemon in half. It is so juicy and overripe, a bit of juice sprays out and hits your eye, giving you a little stinging sensation. After you cut it, you pick up one of the halves, and it's so juicy that some of the juice runs down your hand. Now, imagine taking a big bite of that lemon.

Did you notice at least a tiny reaction, feeling, image, smell, or taste? And yet, there probably aren't even any lemons in the room where you are. Those printed words have been conditioned to create physiological effects. If you didn't speak English, and you were watching someone else do this exercise, you would be wondering why that person had a scrunched-up face. After all, to you, those words would be just scribbly lines or just strange sounds.

In fact, we can repeat the word over and over again to show that it is only a sound. (Make sure you are alone or that your door is closed if you don't want to be embarrassed.) Repeat the word "lemon" out loud, for about 30 seconds. "Lemon, lemon, lemon, lemon, lemon...."

What happened just then?

For most people, it starts to become just a sound again. It just turns into a rhythmic noise.

That is all words ever are—rhythmic noises. It is your brain that puts meaning onto them. The human brain attaches emotions and physiological reactions to these sounds we call words, and then we forget we do it.

Of course, you have to make this point carefully when working with clients. Be careful not to sound like you are making fun of them, because their brains are actually trying to help them with all this thinking. There is no need for them to get mad at their own brains—they can learn to just let the thoughts be there as sounds in their heads. If a client is anxiously obsessed with the thought "I'm a terrible parent," you can ask them to repeat that thought over and over and over again. "I'm a terrible parent. I'm a terrible parent. I'm a terrible parent..." Eventually, the words turn into meaningless noises, like "blah, blah, blah, blah, blah." Then you can compassionately lean toward them and say, "Wow! You're letting these noises tell you how to live your life? Maybe that thought doesn't have to have as much power as your mind has been giving it."

Repeating thoughts out loud can be a kind of exposure therapy. In fact, this is a common technique when using exposure and response prevention for OCD. If a thought won't leave your head, you just literally repeat the thought over and over and over again, until you realize it is just a sound. The sounds start to lose their association with anxiety, and you don't have to try to not think about them anymore.

Repeating thoughts is just one way to promote cognitive defusion.

COGNITIVE DEFUSION: RELATING DIFFERENTLY TO THOUGHTS

Once clients understand how words become fused with meaning and emotion, they can learn the process of defusion. **Defusion refers to the ability to see your thoughts *as* thoughts** (Blackledge, 2007; Hayes, Strosahl, & Wilson, 2012). It is about "stepping back" from the thoughts, or "making room" for them. It involves noticing but not getting caught up in what your thoughts are telling you. Clients can learn to not confuse thoughts with reality. Rather than getting stuck in thoughts, or battling them, they can learn to recognize them as mental events. Sometimes those mental events can be useful, but you don't necessarily have to listen to them or do what they say. They are not your boss.

When children are young, thoughts don't have the reality they have for adults. Once when my youngest daughter was three years old, I was driving her home from school and noticed that it was uncharacteristically quiet in the back seat of the car. Suddenly, I heard her say to herself, "Sorry brain, I'm not going to do what you tell me to do!" I thought to myself, "Good for you honey, don't let that brain boss you around!" She later told me that she had a thought about opening the car door as we were driving down the road. She was able to defuse from it, see that it was just a thought, and she realized that she did not have to act on that thought.

Clients spend a great deal of time worrying and arguing with their own thoughts, so it is a great relief when they realize they don't have to do this. Their energy is then freed up to do so many other things.

I once worked with a client with anxiety who really wanted to take walks in the park, but she told me she just couldn't get herself to do it. In one session, she told me that over the weekend all she did was sit on the couch, thinking that she wanted to walk to the park, but that she just couldn't do it. "You don't understand," she said. "I just cannot get off the couch to go to the park."

I certainly understand that anxiety feels paralyzing, and that it highjacks the thinking process, and that the mind tells you that you cannot do certain things. And yet, she had been getting out and coming to my therapy office like clockwork every week for five years. She'd been going out to the same job for twelve years, and she never missed a day of work without calling in sick or making arrangements. And yet, she couldn't get up off the couch to walk a couple of blocks to the park.

This must be done carefully, because it can sound like you're making fun of your clients if you don't have good rapport with them. I gave this client the following homework assignment. I told her, "This weekend, I want you to sit on your couch, and say out loud over and over, 'I can't walk to the park,' and here is what I want you to do." Then I stood up and moved my feet toward my office door. "I know your anxious feelings are real, but those thoughts are only words, they are just sounds in your head. You get to decide what action to take. You can still move your feet and walk to the park." The client laughed, and she practiced saying it out loud and getting up and walking back and forth in my office.

Most clients think, "Well no, I need to talk myself into being able to walk to the park." It's not like there is an alien invading your head, or a little person in there to whom you are accountable. Thoughts are literally just mental representations of sounds. We have the ability to choose what actions are important to do, even if our thoughts are screaming at us.

There are a lot of ways we can work with defusion, and the following handout gives clients a few of them to consider.

Stepping Back from Anxious Thoughts

Most of us enjoy going to the movies or watching our favorite television programs. When you are watching a movie, you tend to get lost in it, and forget that it is a movie. You can feel scared, excited, sad, and happy, even though the movie is nothing but a series of fast-moving pictures. The people are not even really there! If you step back from the screen, you can remember that it is just a movie, and you don't have to get caught up in all those fears and emotions.

Likewise, **the thoughts in our minds can suck us into worlds that only exist inside our heads**. Our thoughts create strong emotions like anxiety, and we forget that they are only thoughts. When you learn to step back from those thoughts, they begin to lose their power over you.

As an exercise to understand this point, you can write a troublesome thought down on a piece of paper. Maybe the thought is something like "I'm a terrible parent." If you hold that piece of paper up to your face, you will feel stuck to that thought. It will feel like it takes up your entire point of view. If playing with your kids is important to you, it would be pretty tough to do that when you are caught up in this thought.

But what if you could step back from that thought just a little bit, and make more space for the thought? You could do this symbolically by holding the paper out in front of you, a foot or so away. Even if the thought is still there, floating around, and even if you didn't like that thought, couldn't you just get up and go do what you wanted to do, like play with your kids?

Most people want to fight an unpleasant thought. "Get away from me! I don't like this! Go away!" Or, they want to argue back and forth with the thoughts. They might say to their thoughts, "I am too a good parent." And their thoughts might respond with, "*No, you're not. You don't do enough things with your kids.*" "I played with them yesterday." "*That's just because the neighbor was watching.*" Guess what—**while you are fighting or arguing with your thoughts, you are not living your life**. You can practice just noticing, "Oh, look at that, I'm having an argument again with my own thoughts." Then you can choose what you want to do next.

Instead of trying to get rid of the thoughts, you can bring them with you. A thought can't stop you from taking action. A thought can't keep you from playing with your kids. It can't stop you from going to that important family party. It can't stop you from applying for that job. It is just a thought, even if you don't like it. It is just something that is floating through your head. You don't have to fix it. You don't have to argue with it. It just comes out of nowhere, which is what brains do automatically.

Take a few moments right now to write down on a piece of paper a thought that has been bothering you.

What is it that this thought is getting in the way of? In other words, what meaningful thing would you be doing if you weren't spending your time fighting this thought? (For example, if you think you are a terrible parent, and are fighting this thought all the time, maybe you wish you were spending more time playing with the kids.)

Hold the piece of paper up to your face. Feel what it is like to get caught up in this thought. Notice how hard it is to do anything when this is so close to you.

Now move back a little from that piece of paper. Notice that even if the thought is still there, you can see so much more of the world around you. **You can make choices about what you want to do even if the thought is still there.**

I'm sure you wish this thought would just disappear and not bother you anymore. But I'm guessing that has not happened yet, despite all the time you have spent trying to do so. If it is not going away, can you live your life even with that thought floating around?

Symbolically, you can fold up that piece of paper and carry it around with you in your pocket. For the next few days, prove to yourself that you can have that thought and still do the things that are important to you. Instead of arguing with that thought, use that time and energy to live your life.

ACT VERSUS TRADITIONAL CBT

In traditional cognitive therapy, the therapist seeks out and identifies maladaptive or irrational thoughts. The therapist then disputes, challenges, or weighs the evidence for and against those thoughts. However, in component analyses, it appears that **the disputation component of CBT is not essential for it to work** (Longmore & Worrell, 2007). Many therapists find this confusing, because they think that challenging thoughts is the heart of CBT. It appears that in actuality, when you challenge a thought, you have to defuse from it. In other words, when you dispute a thought, you are talking about the thought as a thought, which give you a different perspective on it. Hence, even in traditional CBT, defusion seems to be the effective ingredient. However, in ACT, we de-emphasize the disputation component, because the more you challenge thoughts, the more you are reifying them (Avdagic, Morrissey, & Boschen, 2014; Craske et al., 2014; Sears, 2017a). You are making the thought more real by arguing with it, when it is just a mental event. This is likely why even proponents of traditional CBT tend to de-emphasize direct disputation, preferring instead to use Socratic dialogue (Resick, Monson, & Chard, 2016).

Have you ever had this happen? A client comes to you, and after you do a good and thorough intake assessment, you know exactly what the problem is, since you're a professional and you have seen this a thousand times. Based on your clinical experience and your knowledge of the research literature, you also know exactly what to do for this problem. But when you tell the client what to do, the client says, "Yes, I tried that. It doesn't work." And, because you are a polite person, you then offer another strategy that is effective for the problem. But the client quickly replies, "Yeah, I've tried that too. That doesn't work either." You then immediately offer yet another alternative solution, and you hear, "Yeah, I did that six months ago, and it still doesn't work."

This often happens because you are inadvertently trying to challenge their thoughts with your thoughts. This makes many clients even more deeply entrenched in their thoughts, strengthening their tendency to defensively fight back with yet more argumentative thinking. When you notice this happening, you can defuse from the thinking. "Notice how your mind keeps telling you that nothing works. I bet you have tried so many things that you feel pretty hopeless right now that things will ever get better." In this example, the deeper issue may be the feeling of hopelessness.

As mentioned in chapter 2, there's a phenomenon that helps explain why clients can fire back so many anxiety-related thoughts when they are anxious. It is called mood state-dependent learning and memory (Ucros, 1989). When you are in a certain mood state, your brain automatically fires up thoughts and memories related to that mood state. So, when you are anxious, your brain quickly and easily lights up memories of other times you've been anxious and is more likely to activate worrisome thoughts about yourself, the world, and the future. This is just the way the human brain is wired. It can be difficult to access happy or realistic thoughts when you are in an anxious mood.

By the way, the opposite is true too. Do you have one of those annoyingly happy friends? Because they are almost always in a happy mood, they continuously spout out happy thoughts and memories. It takes an unhappy event or shift in mood to knock them out of that happy state before they can access other, less positive thoughts and memories.

When clients come to you, they do not realize that all these thought wars are being waged against themselves. It is like the left hand and right hand are having a tug of war. They want me to help them pull harder on the side that is creating the good thoughts, not realizing that it only makes the other side pull harder with negative thoughts. Our job is to whisper in their ears, "Both of those hands are yours!" It is such an odd feeling for them to just let go. They have battled for so long that they keep thinking they need to try harder and harder. They experience such relief when they finally learn to let go of this battle.

Of course, ACT can incorporate CBT techniques in the sense that if they work, and help clients move toward their values, they are useful. Isn't it wonderful when you are able to reframe something for a client, and you notice a big shift? You toss out an amazing new way of thinking about something, saying, "Well, have you ever thought about it this way?" You see the client pause, a light bulb goes off, and it changes their life forever. Fantastic! It's the stuff therapists dream about.

Unfortunately, more often you find that clients just continue arguing with you or with themselves. This is why ACT and other third-wave approaches emphasize defusion. In fact, CBT calls this process "distancing," noticing your thoughts as thoughts, rather than getting caught up in the thoughts or battling with them. While I am not necessarily suggesting you should never challenge a client's thoughts, it is important to keep in mind that the actual mechanism is defusion. When you challenge a client's thoughts, it helps them uncouple their thoughts from the automaticity of their associated meanings and emotions. ACT de-emphasizes thought disputation, since doing so often results in arguments and battles, giving thoughts more power.

This defusion process is likely an important ingredient in all talk therapy, since discussing thoughts out loud helps defuse from them. It is probably also an important reason that journaling, or writing thoughts down on paper, is so helpful for clients (Pennebaker, 1997).

There are many exercises for helping clients let go of their struggles with their anxious thoughts. In the "thought trains exercise" (Hayes, Strosahl, & Wilson, 2012), clients can practice noticing how quickly trains of thought pull them away from the moment, with an anxious thought leading to another anxious thought leading to another. Rather than trying to stop the thought trains, or battle with them, clients can learn to just observe them.

Thought Trains Exercise

Our brains can be very busy places, sometimes busier than Grand Central Station. Trains of thought can carry us off to all sorts of far-off locations. Sometimes the brain's ability to go off to strange places can be a good thing. It is called creativity. But if you have anxiety, your mind likely goes off to faraway places that are not helpful.

For example, I recently saw a news story that 22 people had been killed in a severe tornado. Since my family recently moved into a home with no basement, it reminded me that I need to think about a severe weather safety plan. But if I was feeling overly anxious about it, those thoughts could have gone into far-off destinations, where one thought leads to another like a runaway train.

If you have a lot of anxiety, even thoughts that start off in Happytown can easily end up in Anxietyville. "It's such a nice day today. But what if it doesn't last? What if the weather forecast is wrong? They certainly are wrong a lot. What if it gets windy and stormy? I'm still not prepared for a tornado. What if my house gets blown away? What if I never recover from that? What if I'm so distraught I lose my job and become penniless and homeless?"

"What If" Railroads definitely provides regular non-stop service to Anxietyville. Even a thought like "It's such a nice day today" can take you to worrying about being penniless and homeless.

When you are on one of these anxiety thought trains, you may metaphorically feel shaken up and jostled around. But if you view the trains from above, you can peacefully watch them go on down the tracks. Likewise, when you are lost in your anxious thoughts, you feel the anxiety intensely. But when you can step back and just see your thoughts as thoughts, and don't confuse them with the reality they are trying to represent, the struggle connected with those thoughts begins to drop away.

You may not be able to stop these trains, but you can learn to not let them take you for a ride. You don't have to stay on the trains. You can learn to step off and watch them go by. Instead of worrying all day, you can consciously choose if, when, and how you want to think about a real problem like a weather safety plan. You will likely find that more anxiety trains keep coming along, but you don't have to jump on board any of those either.

When first learning this skill, it is best to practice it in a quiet place. As you get better at doing this, you can do it anytime throughout the day, and you will be able to notice when your mind goes off to irrelevant places more often. The concept is very simple: Notice when you are being pulled away by a thought train, and rise up above it. Of course, simple is not necessarily easy, so it takes practice.

Find a peaceful place to sit or lie down. Close your eyes, or you can just shade them and keep them slightly open. Take a few deep breaths, and let yourself settle into a comfortable position.

Begin to notice any thoughts that are going on in your mind. Some thoughts may be loud and obvious, other thoughts may be barely noticeable. Sometimes you might not be aware of any thoughts at all.

Imagine these thoughts as trains. When you are lost in the thought, it will feel like you are on the train. When you notice yourself being carried away, imagine you can rise up above the train and view it from the sky. See if you can just watch the trains of thought going by.

When you find yourself inside a thought, like "I'm just never going to stop being anxious," see if you can rise above it, and just notice, "Ah, there goes the thought 'I'm just never going to stop being anxious'" and let it roll on down the tracks. You don't necessarily need words to describe the process, just practice having the experience of stepping back from the thoughts.

When you are on a thought train, you may not realize it at first. One thought leads to another, leads to another, leads to another, and leads to another. The point is just to practice noticing when that happens, even if you have already been taken a few miles down the tracks.

When you notice that you have been taken for a ride, imagine that you can rise above the trains. Picture yourself up in the sky, watching the train go on wherever it wants to go. Notice that thought train as separate from you, just doing what it does.

Sooner or later, you are likely to get pulled back onto that thought train again, or perhaps onto another one. Whenever you notice yourself caught up in and carried away by your thoughts, practice rising back up again.

Eventually, you may be able to notice multiple thought trains chugging along at the same time. Sometimes their tracks may even cross.

You may find yourself automatically wanting to argue with or get rid of particular thoughts. While there are times you may need to think about certain things, for this exercise, it is important to keep an attitude of curiosity, and even humor. See if you can let go of struggles or attempts to control or stop the thoughts. Trying to stop a freight train is only going to wear you out (or get you run over!). It is much easier to get off a train and observe it.

With practice, you may even be able to drop the train metaphor, and just notice your thoughts as they are. You will be able to choose when and if you want to go off with them, or if you just want to step back and observe them as they are.

Even practicing this exercise a few minutes a day can help you shift how you relate to your thoughts. When you do need to problem solve real-life issues, you will do so much more effectively when your mind is not automatically pulled in a dozen different directions.

Tip for Clinicians ————————————————————————

Should you use the words fusion and defusion with clients? It depends on the clients with whom you work, and if you think it would be helpful or confusing. Many of my clients can relate to the metaphor of being "fused" to a thought, so the word "defusion" makes sense to them. Others seem to relate better to certain thoughts being "sticky," and that we can practice making room for the thoughts to get "unstuck" from them. As you gain experience, you will begin to find a variety of ways to explain defusion to a diverse range of clients.

As another way to practice defusion, the following exercise is called "physicalizing" (Hayes, 2007; Hayes, Strosahl, & Wilson, 2012). Many of you will recognize this as something often done by Gestalt therapists. When clients are fused with thoughts, they end up lost in their heads in endless battles. By putting a thought out in front of them, and imagining what physical attributes it might have, they are stepping back and getting some perspective on it. The point is not to push it away, but to learn to relate to it differently. While it may be best to read this worksheet to the client the first time they do it so they can focus on the process, clients can practice doing this on their own at home.

Putting Your Thoughts
Out in Front of You

Everyone experiences anxious thoughts. It is a natural part of being alive. These thoughts can help you solve problems and help you decide what actions to take when something important needs to be done.

But since anxious thoughts tend to be unpleasant, we often develop ways of trying to get rid of them, to ignore them, or to push them away. Unfortunately, this can often lead to the thoughts growing bigger and bigger in our minds over time. This makes us even more reluctant to be with them, and we try harder and harder to fight with them or to keep them out of our minds.

Ignoring these thoughts has probably not been working for you, at least not more than temporarily. It is important to get to know these thoughts, these processes to which you may have given control of your life. In this exercise, we are going to practice stepping back from the thoughts to get a broader perspective on them.

First of all, let's get the thoughts out of the shadows and into the spotlight. Be specific: What are the most common anxious thoughts you have? Common ones include: "What if something goes wrong?," "Nobody will ever love me," "What if I get sick?," "If I go to the party, I'll do something embarrassing," or "If I leave the house, I'll have a panic attack."

Make a list of some of the most common anxious thoughts you have, the ones that bother you the most:

_____

_____

_____

_____

_____

_____

_____

_____

As you sit with the questions below, your logical, thinking mind might think this is weird or corny. You may wonder how this could possibly help. It's the mind's job to protect you, so thank your mind and go back to doing the exercise as best you can. If you want things to be different in your life, you will need to be willing to do something different.

Ideally, find a quiet, comfortable place where you won't be interrupted. Notice what your mind does as you settle into the place you are—it will likely keep trying to distract you. That's okay—it's just trying to help again. Notice where your mind goes and practice bringing your attention back to the exercise.

Pick one of the thoughts from the list you made earlier. Imagine that this thought takes physical form and is floating in the air about 10 feet out in front of you.

If it had a size, how big would this thought be?

_____

If it had a shape, what shape would this thought be?

_____

If it had a color, what color would this thought be?

_____

If it had a speed, how fast would this thought be moving?

_____

If it had a smell, what would this thought smell like?

_____

If it had a weight, how heavy would this thought be?

_____

If it had a level of power, how much power would this thought have to push you around?

_____

Continue to observe this vision of the thought out in front you for a few minutes. If you find this challenging, just do the best you can. As you watch it, ask yourself the following questions:

How much power, time, and energy have you been giving to this thought?

_____

_____

_____

As you look at this thought, seeing its shape, color, size, and speed, is it really something that is going to destroy you? Is this something that demands you constantly fight with it? Do you really need to spend so much of your time and energy trying to push it away?

_____

_____

Is this thing worth giving up your life for? Do you really want to give up on your values for this thing?

_____

_____

If it meant that you could live a more fulfilling life, whatever that means to you, would you be willing to allow this thing to be exactly as it is? Of course you don't like it, but would you be willing to allow it to be your companion if it meant you could do more of the things that matter to you?

_____

_____

Pay close attention to what your mind does with this next question:

Are you willing to take that thought back now? To be with it and hold it, even if you don't like what it says? In some ways, this old companion of yours has tried to help you, to protect you. Could you imagine embracing it as if it were a child or friend that you love, even if they were covered in mud and smelly? Or, would you be willing to imagine shrinking or folding up that anxiety, and sticking it in your pocket? Not as something you are, but as something you can carry with you?

_____

_____

If the answer to the above question is yes, just spend a few more minutes with this thought, this old, familiar companion of yours.

If the answer to the above question is no, continue with the next questions.

Get in touch with the resistance, fear, and/or hesitancy to take this thought back. Imagine moving your visualization of the thought off to one side, then imagine this resistance out in front of you.

If it had a size, how big would your resistance be?

_____

If it had a shape, what shape would your resistance be?

_____

If it had a color, what color would your resistance be?

_____

If it had a speed, how fast would your resistance be moving?

_____

If it had a smell, what would your resistance smell like?

_____

If it had a weight, how heavy would your resistance be?

_____

If it had a level of power, how much power would it have to push you around?

_____

As you look at this resistance, seeing its shape, color, size, and speed, is it really something that is going to destroy you? Is this something that demands you constantly fight with it? Does it really need you to spend time and energy pushing it away?

_____

_____

Is this thing worth giving up your life for? Do you really want to give up on your values for this thing?

_____

_____

If it meant that you could live a more fulfilling life, whatever that means to you, would you be willing to allow this thing to be exactly as it is? Of course you don't like it, but would you be willing to allow it to be your companion if it meant you could do more of the things that matter to you?

_____

_____

Again, pay close attention to what your mind does with this next question:

Are you willing to take that resistance back now? To be with it and hold it, even if you don't like it? In some ways, this old companion of yours has tried to help you, to protect you. Could you imagine embracing it as if it were a child or friend that you love, even if they were covered in mud and smelly? Or, would you be willing to imagine shrinking or folding up that resistance, and sticking it in your pocket? Not as something you are, but as something you can carry with you?

_____

_____

If the answer to the above question is no, then repeat the exercise about taking back the resistance. If the answer is yes, then go back to the question about taking back the thought.

You can repeat this exercise as often as you like, and you can do it with all of the anxious thoughts on your list.

You have probably spent many years ignoring, battling, or pushing away your thoughts, so be patient with yourself as you practice this exercise. Consider this exercise as an experiment in doing things differently, and see if you can suspend your expectations and judgments about whether or not you are doing it "right."

SHIFTING FROM CONTENT TO PROCESS

Another way to view defusion is as a shift from the content of the thoughts to the process of thinking. Shifting from content to process is something we do frequently in all types of psychotherapy, and it is especially important in group therapy (Yalom & Leszcz, 2005).

When you are a new group therapist, you tend to think that the content of what clients are talking about is the most important thing, and you can get overly caught up in worrying about "losing control" of the session. For example, imagine you are conducting an interpersonal growth type of group. In the very first session, a client who has been in therapy groups for decades immediately begins to disclose all the intimate details of his sexual trauma history, and all the other clients in the group shift around nervously. A new group therapist in that situation might get really nervous and try to find something wise to say about the sexual trauma history itself, which is pretty difficult to do without any background information.

Of course, when in doubt, you can always shift to process. "Wow! The fact that you are telling us all such meaningful personal information right now tells me that you feel really safe in this group. But given that this is our very first meeting, I'm not sure that everyone else in the room feels that safe. What can we do as a group to make this a safe place so that we can get beyond superficial stuff and talk about things that are really important?"

See how I did that? I just shifted from the content of the disclosure to the process of disclosing. In all the years I've been a psychologist, working with thousands of clients, I have never yet had someone say, "Hold on a second! I see the trick you just did! You shifted from content to process, and I want to go back to my content!" If you tell a client that talking about that content is not appropriate, they will feel like they have been shut down. But doing it this way helps the client feel heard and validated. Of course, clients may indeed go back to talking about the content again. In that case, you can simply say, "Isn't it interesting how we just keep going back to that topic? I wonder why we can't let it go?"

Now it's possible in group therapy situations that everyone ends up getting lost in processing the process, and no one gets into any of the important content. In that case, we can choose to move back into content. Being able to shift back and forth allows us to modulate how deeply we go into things.

Likewise, we can shift from the content of thoughts to the process of thinking. A client may have a thought, like "I'm just not going to be able to do this." Instead of arguing, the therapist can say, "Okay, so you are noticing those thoughts coming up that you're not going to be able to do this. Are you willing to just do it anyway?"

A client is likely to immediately reply, "I just don't think it's going to work."

"Okay, so you're noticing the thought that it may not work, but are you willing to just do it anyway, because you told me this was really important to you?"

Do you see how different that is from "Well, evidence shows that this does work, so I think you should give it a try"? The client is then likely to say, "Well, it won't work for me." Clients are often very practiced at arguing with the content of verbal processes. You may certainly need to discuss content at times, but for those clients who are really stuck, you can shift attention to the process of thinking. It is a way of sidestepping the thoughts rather than taking them head-on.

When people are experiencing strong anxiety, it is hard to talk them out of anxious thoughts. They find lots of reasons why their thoughts are true, why they will never get better, or why they think they are terrible people. There is no need to argue with the content. "Okay, so you are noticing a thought again that you are a terrible person. Sounds like Mr. Anxiety is talking."

Personifying the thinking, or using a metaphor for the thinking process, is another way of shifting from content to process to facilitate defusion (Hayes, Strosahl, & Wilson, 2012). "Hmm, it sounds like 'Radio Doom and Gloom' is back on the air, telling you that nothing is ever going to work. Tell me, when you've listened to 'Radio Doom and Gloom' in the past, how has that improved your life?"

The client might realize, "Well, it makes me stay home, and then I'm lonely."

"Okay, so maybe when 'Radio Doom and Gloom' starts playing, you don't have to listen to that. You can just go out anyway if it's important to you."

We can also let clients know that the brain is "a reason-giving machine." That's what it is designed to do. Sometimes it is useful, sometimes not, but you don't have to fight it or stop it. You can respond to your own brain with compassion. "Ah, thank you brain. You are trying to give me some helpful advice. I appreciate your input, but I'm going to do this important thing anyway."

We can also describe the brain as a judgment factory (Bach & Moran, 2008), which is the topic of the next worksheet.

The Judgment Factory

Judgments can be very important in our practical, day-to-day lives. They help us make choices. They help us solve problems. They help us decide what to do in the context of our circumstances. They help us prepare for what might go wrong in the future.

But do you sometimes find it difficult to just enjoy things as they are, even when things are going well? Do you notice yourself making judgments all the time, out of habit?

Your brain is a judgment factory. It cranks out comparisons all the time. That's what it's designed to do. It continuously compares what is happening here and now to some other time and place. If your job requires you to make constant judgments, it might be a useful skill at work. However, while you are making judgments, you are not experiencing reality in this moment as fully—your attention is off in your head. This is why it becomes hard to just be in the moment and enjoy it as it is.

The good news is you don't have to argue with these judgments. After all, there is not a separate person in your head that you have to answer back to. There is also no need to try to stop these judgments, which is good to know, because they will likely just keep coming up automatically anyway from time to time. **What you can learn to do is not engage with them or give them more power when they do show up.**

Siddhartha Gautama once asked, "If someone offers you a tray of filth, and you do not take it, who is left holding it?" You may not like it, and it may even smell bad to have it near you, but fighting with or trying to push away that tray will probably just cause the filth to fall all over you. Then you'll be tired, sweaty, smelly, and covered with filth.

The judgments our brains produce can be pretty nasty as well. You don't have to like them. Yet, struggling and arguing with them tends to stir them up all the more. It's not necessarily about ignoring them either, because like a kid throwing a temper tantrum, they often get louder. What you can practice doing (and this does take practice!) is just letting them be there. You don't have to fight them, you don't have to push them away, and you don't have to grit your teeth and "endure" them. Just notice, "Ah, here is the judgment factory again," decide whether or not they are actually helpful or just old filth, and choose what you want to do in this moment. What really matters in your life? How can you move toward those things, even with the judgments around?

Take a few moments to consider the questions below. Pay careful attention to what your mind does as you are doing this. Go through this worksheet several times to see how or if your answers change over time.

What kinds of judgments does your factory often pump out about yourself?

_____

_____

_____

_____

What kinds of judgments does your factory often pump out about other people?

_____

_____

_____

_____

What kinds of judgments does your factory often pump out about the world?

_____

_____

_____

_____

What kinds of judgments does your factory often pump out about the past and the future?

_____

_____

_____

_____

What have you tried to do in the past when these judgments have come up? (argue with them, ignore them, distract yourself, etc.)

_____

_____

_____

_____

What are these judgments getting in the way of? What do you want to do more of or have more of in your life?

_____

_____

_____

_____

Would you be willing to spend less time fighting and struggling with these judgments, and spend more time doing what matters to you?

_____

_____

_____

_____

What is one thing you can do today that would be meaningful or enjoyable, even if the judgments show up?

_____

_____

_____

_____

The more often you notice these judgments, the less power they will have over you. It's like watching horror movies: The first few times you see them, they bother you, but after seeing them hundreds of times, they don't bother you at all. Even if you can't stop the movies from playing, they don't have to affect you emotionally. The more you notice what your judgment factory pumps out, the less power those judgments will have over you.

Tip for Clinicians

Watch out, because clients will try to pull you into their judgments and their thought battles. They want you to argue with their thoughts, and since this is what they do all day long, they will easily come up with strong counterpoints. By talking about the process of thinking, we can sort of step outside of the struggle, and this models defusion for clients. "I'm noticing how every time this topic comes up, these thoughts come back. You brain just can't help it." For example, for a client who is anxious about dating, you might say, "Because of your history, every time you think about going on a date, you're going to think the person is going to cheat on you. That is just what your brain does. It is automatically going to make that judgment. Are you willing to go ahead and make that phone call or go on that first date anyway?"

It is wonderful when clients start to really understand defusion. They often say that after wasting so many years inside their heads, they begin appreciating the moments of their lives. Of course, thinking is often very valuable, but life is meant to be experienced, not figured out. An analogy that clients often find helpful is Kelly Wilson's question about math problems and sunsets (Wilson & DuFrene, 2009), as described in the following worksheet.

Math Problem or Sunset?

Psychologist Kelly Wilson liked to ask his supervisees, "Do you see your clients as a math problem, or as a sunset?"

I think this is an important question to ask about all our relationships, and about life itself. J. J. van der Leeuw (1928) once said, "The mystery of life is not a problem to be solved; it is a reality to be experienced."

There are times we need to solve problems. We sometimes need to calculate and strategize in words to get to a solution. But you don't "solve" a sunset. It is not a problem. It is something to be experienced.

When you have anxiety, you tend to overthink things. So many things in life become math problems to be solved, or things to be analyzed. There is an almost infinite variety of possible future issues than can arise, and the brain wants to try to plan and prepare for all of them. It can become easy to get in the habit of seeing everything as a problem, and to lose the ability to just enjoy our moments.

Also, if you've had challenging relationships, you may begin to treat your relationships as math problems. You may find yourself constantly trying to fix or analyze the people you care about. While there may be very real issues you need to figure out, humans are also marvelously complex and beautiful beings. Can you sometimes set aside the analysis, and just enjoy their presence? Are there moments that you can just be present with, as you would a sunset?

What are some things you are currently approaching as a math problem? Take some time to consider a variety of things that may not even be apparent at first. You might include such things as relationships, your home, eating habits, music, and hobbies. In what way might you be treating these or other things as math problems?

_____

_____

_____

_____

_____

_____

_____

_____

How can you take more of a sunset approach to each of these things? What wonders are within each of these things that can be appreciated rather than analyzed?

_____

_____

_____

_____

_____

_____

_____

_____

What is one thing you can approach more like a sunset today? How would you be different as you do that? What might you do or say in a different way? (For example, taking a deep breath and smiling when you first wake up or see a friend, rather than immediately going into problem-solving mode.)

_____

_____

_____

_____

_____

_____

_____

Pick one thing, situation, or relationship each day that you can approach more as a sunset, even if only for a few moments. Over time, you may just find many more sunsets than math problems in your life.

As with all of the ACT processes, defusion is deeply intertwined with the other five. It is about seeing yourself as more than just your thoughts. You can only notice your thoughts in the present moment. Stepping back from thoughts allows you to more clearly see where you're going in life, and what steps you want to take to get there. When clients are less caught up in their thinking, they are more free to experience the richness of their emotions, and to see reality as it is. In the next chapter, we will explore acceptance.

Chapter

6

Acceptance: Letting Go of the Battle with Anxious Feelings

Clients with anxiety spend inordinate amounts of time struggling with reality and trying not to feel their unpleasant emotions. They get stuck wishing the past would have been different, or they regret all the wasted years they avoided living their lives. Their lives pass them by as they imagine all the worst possibilities of what might happen in the future, or they put off living now for the sake of an imagined future in which everything settles down and the anxiety disappears.

If you want to build a life worth living, you can only start from where you are. **Letting go of struggles with emotions, and accepting reality as it is in this moment, frees you to focus on the actions you can take right now to build a life worth living.** You may not be able to control your thoughts or feelings, but you can choose what you do in this moment.

CLEAN ANXIETY VERSUS DIRTY ANXIETY

Sometimes people get the mistaken idea that the goal is to have no anxiety or strong emotions of any kind. I have been around a number of so-called mindfulness or meditation teachers that speak in a monotone voice as if they have no emotions, and are always in a state of perfect equanimity. Then I will see them yelling at the cashier later on for getting their order wrong.

If you've struggled with anxiety your whole life, you might think, "Wouldn't it be nice to just never feel anything?" Of course not! That's like being a stone. To have emotions, to have compassion, and to feel what other people are feeling is the richness of being human. We want that. We just don't want to get stuck in those emotions.

For clients, it can be useful to distinguish "clean" anxiety from "dirty" anxiety (Hayes, Strosahl, & Wilson, 2012), and this concept applies to all emotions. Clean emotions are the natural and spontaneous feelings, memories, and thoughts that are just going to show up if you are living life. If you're going to live life fully, you're just going to have anxiety come up sometimes.

Dirty anxiety is what shows up when you are attempting to control or avoid the things that come up as a natural part of life. We could call it, "anxiety about anxiety." Instead of just having the anxiety, people tend to get caught up in battling with it. For example, anticipatory anxiety is the fear of being anxious in the future, which triggers more anxiety in the present.

Rather than trying to fight it, control it, or avoid it, clients can learn to recognize that anxiety is a part of being alive. In fact, there are benefits to having anxiety, as discussed in the next handout.

The Benefits of Anxiety

I'm sure that if you're reading this, you want less anxiety in your life. You might even wish you had no anxiety. While I don't want to minimize how bad things have been for you, for just a moment, I want you to imagine a life without anxiety.

At first, you might think that would be wonderful!

However, even so-called negative emotions like anxiety are very useful if we don't get stuck in them. **Anxiety gives us information**. It is often a very useful messenger.

For example, once when I was about to give a two-day public workshop, I realized I had forgotten the power cord for my laptop. Now, even though I have given literally hundreds of workshops, and it is very common for problems like this to arise, I still had some anxiety when there was no power cord for my laptop.

This may sound like a funny thing to say, but in that situation, I *wanted* to have that little bit of anxiety. Just imagine if I had no anxiety, with an attitude like "Yeah, whatever. I've already seen the slides and the videos. I don't care if the audience sees them." I wouldn't do anything about the missing power cord if I had zero anxiety. That anxiety is a messenger, basically telling me, "Hey—this is important. You want the audience to see your slides and videos in order to get this information to them more effectively. You better do some problem solving." The anxiety motivated me to put my laptop in a power saving mode, and then I went and bought a new power cord during the lunch break, and then the anxiety went away. That's what it is designed to do: to give you a message. Instead of struggling with it, you can just receive the message, even though you don't like it. **The feelings in your body are just giving you a message.**

Now, by definition, no human being likes feeling anxiety—otherwise you would call it "excitement." But can you imagine what would happen in that situation if I made the anxiety itself the problem? I could leave the room, sit down, and do a relaxation technique. I could close my eyes and imagine myself at the beach, and I might even be able to lower the anxiety. But as soon as I opened my eyes and went back into the room, there would still be no power cord!

In this example, it is obvious that the anxiety itself is not the problem, it is a messenger. It is something my body is doing to give me information. Sometimes that information might be old information from the past, or from previous conditioning, and may have little to do with the present situation. It may or may not be useful, but either way, I don't have to fight the messenger. The anxiety is not the real problem. But if I keep fighting the anxiety, it can spiral into a much bigger problem.

You might think it would be great if you could be happy all the time, but life doesn't work that way. Have you ever met somebody who tries to be happy all the time? They often end up being miserable, because they are trying to force their feelings to stay a certain way. Their attempts to always be happy can upset the people around them. For example, if your dog died, you would not want someone to say, "Well, look at the bright side, at least your cat didn't die. Be happy!" That would be totally inappropriate! You would want compassion. You would want to hear, "I'm so sorry! I had a dog once, and I just bawled like a baby in the vet's office when he died!" That is human. We want to be able to feel, we just don't want to get stuck in our feelings.

Believe it or not, I've even seen the Dalai Lama angry, but he doesn't stew on it for months, or plot revenge. If one of his assistants is creating a problem, he may forcefully tell him to stop it. But then in the next moment, he may smile and give a hug to a visitor. His emotions are what give meaning to his words, and he does not permanently get stuck in any one emotion.

Are you willing to feel uncomfortable sometimes in the service of what matters to you? If you wait until you feel better to live your life, you could be waiting a long time. You can build that life now, even if you are currently feeling anxiety. **When we learn to let go of the struggles with our emotions, we can use that energy to take some action steps.** We can eventually learn that emotions like anxiety can even make our lives much richer.

EXPERIENTIAL AVOIDANCE

Experiential avoidance is the opposite of acceptance and leads to inflexibility. It refers to the tendency to want to avoid or push away unpleasant experiences. This can take the form of internal avoidance or external avoidance. Internal avoidance involves trying to get away from internal experiences, like unpleasant thoughts, memories, and feelings like anxiety. External avoidance involves running away from external situations that might trigger those internal experiences, like someone with social anxiety avoiding crowds because they don't like how they feel when they are around strangers. It may also take the form of denying reality, spending precious time wishing things were different than they are in the moment, and getting stuck in thinking of an ideal past or an imagined future, rather than living and creating a meaningful life now.

From a very young age, we are expected to "control" our feelings, as if we even could. Parents and caregivers often say confusing things to their children. If a tiny child falls and scrapes a knee, she is likely to cry, but her parent might say, "Stop crying—you're not hurt!" What is the child to make of this? She sees blood on her knee and knows that's not normal. She feels her knee stinging, with pulsating sensations shooting up her leg. She feels her body heaving and her face wet from crying. Yet, this giant person who loves her, feeds her, protects her, and knows everything tells her she is not hurt. She begins to doubt her own perceptions and feelings, and thinks that there must be some kind of switch to turn off or control her feelings when they are inconvenient to herself or others.

Even as adults, we often try to forcibly control our feelings. You may be going through a horrible life crisis, but you are expected to put on a professional face at work. If you express your feelings too much, your mental health is questioned.

This attempt to control our feelings leads to a lifelong sense of struggle. Instead of just experiencing them, we battle with them. When a thought pops up about how terrible we are, we think about how terrible we are for thinking we are terrible. When our bodies hurt, we tense up against our pain. When we feel stress, we get stressed out. We feel anxious about our anxiety. We get depressed about our depression. We grieve over our grief. We feel ashamed of our shame. We feel guilty about our guilt.

When we are raised with the idea that anxiety and other strong emotions are bad, we develop a habit of struggling with ourselves. We fight our emotions, push them down, or ignore them. Yet our "success" at doing this is temporary at best. Emotions are just not things we can consciously control. We can influence them, and we can suppress them for a little while, but you can't turn them on and off like you are flipping a switch.

Steven Hayes (2007) gives an example. Imagine if I were to hold a gun to your head right now, and you had a very sophisticated polygraph machine attached to you. Then, I said, "If you show any signs of anxiety, I am going to pull this trigger. But if you're not anxious about this at all, I won't kill you." Do you think you could be completely without any anxiety in that moment, with a gun pointed at you? Maybe, if you had been trained as some kind of cold-blooded killer, but chances are you would become anxious. Your body just reacts. That's what it does. You can't control it or change it even when your life depends on it! In fact, you may have felt a little anxiety just reading this, without a real threat even being present!

Hence, clients can learn that all the time and energy they spend battling or avoiding their own emotions not only doesn't work long term, but that these struggles take energy and time away from doing the things in their lives that really matter to them. When they let go of avoidance, they can open up to new ways to relating to their anxiety.

In the following handout, the topic of control is introduced to clients, along with the idea of "riding the waves" of the anxiety.

Riding the Waves of Anxiety

You may not want to hear this, but you will never completely get rid of anxiety. It comes with being human, and there are times when it actually enriches our lives. While of course no one wants to be anxious all the time, ironically, fighting and trying to control the anxiety often makes it worse.

Everyone feels some degree of anxiety. Recently, I got an email from my local airport, where I had just rented an airplane to take my family flying. The message was from the manager, stating that he had received a report of a potential safety violation involving my flight the previous weekend, and he wanted me to call and give my side of the story. My heart began racing, and anxiety flowed through my body. My mind began reeling with thoughts. What could I have done? Did I miss an item on the checklist and cause a problem with the plane? Did my two passengers exceed the weight and balance limitations of the aircraft? Were they going to suspend my rental privileges? Was this just the airport's internal reporting, or was this something being reported to the Federal Aviation Administration?

Of course, all those thoughts increased my anxiety, which increased my anxious thinking. Thoughts actually popped up to give up flying, to stop reading my airplane magazines each night, and to give up on my dream of someday building my own airplane.

Fortunately, I know how anxiety works. I just watched these thoughts come and go. I just felt the anxiety, knowing I could not "control" it. All I could control was my actions. I called the airport immediately, but of course the person was not there, so I left a message. They did not call me back until the next day. While I was waiting, I rechecked my weight and balance calculations and found that I was operating within limits, and just let myself have the anxiety.

When the manager called me, it was because the person who gave me the aircraft keys saw that there were three people with me that day, and the aircraft I was renting could only support two passengers in addition to the pilot. A previous renter had overloaded another airplane the previous week and sustained severe damage on landing. (I did remember seeing a broken-down airplane on the side of the runway that day.) The manager wanted to clarify that I understood the weight limitations of the aircraft, and we had a good conversation, after which I immediately felt relieved.

Here's my point: I am a clinical psychologist and a Zen teacher, and I still had automatic thoughts and anxiety coming up over something that was fairly minor in the big picture of things. There is no need to beat yourself up about having anxious thoughts or to get anxious about getting anxiety. You may be dealing with some very real, very scary things right now, but fighting yourself won't help. Let go of trying to control your thoughts and feelings, decide what is most important to you in your life, and take small action steps.

Rather than fighting your anxiety, you can learn to ride the waves as it comes and goes. Recently, I went white water rafting with my family. It created anxiety, but it was also thrilling. Before we got into the rafts, we prepared by watching a video. We learned what to do if we fell in the water, and we had a guide to watch out for us.

Before we entered the Class 3 rapids, there was a lot of trepidation. When we were in the waves, there was a combination of excitement and fear. Afterward, we were thrilled.

You can choose to sit on the shore, but that choice will come with a cost. If you choose to get in the water, life will be much richer. If you do choose to go down the stream of life, you cannot control the water itself. It is natural to be apprehensive about the waves you see coming up. It is also natural to be unhappy when you are caught in the waves. And, it is natural to be happy when the waves are over. Give yourself permission to feel all these feelings. Rather than gritting your teeth through the whole thing, you can learn to ride the waves.

ACCEPTANCE OF REALITY

Acceptance is of course a very important part of ACT, and it is often very misunderstood. Normally, when we say, "I accept that," there is an implication that you are sort of okay with it. As we are using the word here, you may not be okay with it at all. You may be experiencing a horrible tragedy and might not like anything about it. In this context, **acceptance means accepting reality as it is in this moment, whether you like it or not.** In fact, the popular expression "it is what it is" is a pretty good definition of acceptance.

If you do not acknowledge how things really are in this moment, how can you possibly change them? If we spend inordinate amounts of time bemoaning how things are, ranting about how unfair something is, or angrily holding on to past hurts, we are only wasting energy. That energy is better spent doing something proactive to change things, if it is possible to do so. If it is something that cannot be changed, there is no point in wishing it were otherwise.

We can only ever start from where we are right now. Alan Watts (2004) once told a story about a man who was lost in the English countryside, trying to find an obscure village. When the man finally went up to a local to ask the way, the local said, "Well sir, I do know the way, but if I were you, I wouldn't start from here!"

While it is a silly joke, the above story can help us understand the problems that arise when we lack acceptance of reality. The lost traveler could easily and understandably complain about how unfair it is that he is lost, how it was his travel agent's fault, how there should be more road signs, and how the phone company should have put up more cell towers to give him better reception. The traveler may be absolutely justified in his complaining, but **until he accepts the reality of where he actually is in that moment, how can he possibly get to where he wants to go?** He could spend his whole life complaining and end up going nowhere.

Of course, we know that clients are often told to "just get over it" or to "just get on with your life," which tends not to be very helpful. Past emotions and traumas may need to be processed. But what a tragedy that clients get so stuck in the past that they lose the capacity to live in this moment, even if the present does contain painful memories.

Acceptance does not mean resignation. It does not mean that you just curl up in a ball and feel completely hopeless. You may well do everything in your power in the next moment to make things different if you can, but there is no way you can do or fix anything if you cannot get in touch with the way things are right now.

A client once came into my office and said something to the effect of "I'm in a bad relationship, and I need you to help me accept it better." I suspect she must have read a book about acceptance and misunderstood what that word really meant.

As an important aside, as soon as I heard this client say, "bad relationship," a little red flag went off in my mind, as I hope it did for you. I considered the possibility of domestic violence. It is very important for all clinicians to get training in domestic and family violence, as it has a way of rearing its ugly head into all kinds of situations, even though you might not think you will ever encounter it. The things that seem like common sense based on most people's clinical training can actually harm clients in a domestic violence situation. Even when physical violence is present, the average person leaves eight or nine times before they can permanently end the relationship. You need to understand why that happens so you do not shame the client into quitting therapy. If you do not understand the dynamics of the power and control issues involved, of the economic manipulation, the isolation, and the shaming that occurs, you will probably only cause more frustration. The most dangerous time for the client is right after they leave the relationship, when they are statistically most likely to be hurt or even killed.

For this particular client, it turned out that there were no power and control issues. When she said, "bad relationship," she meant that it was unfulfilling or unsatisfying. Acceptance does not mean you are okay with things, or that you don't want to change them. If I could put the words in her mouth, perhaps this is what she really meant to say: "I've discovered that I'm in another unfulfilling relationship again. When I look back over my life, I see that there have been a whole series of unsatisfying relationships, and it has dawned on me that I am the common denominator in all these bad relationships. I really don't want to accept that I've done this again. What I want to believe is that if only I said the right things, if only we spent more time together, or if only I could give him all the love he never got as a child, then this would blossom into the relationship I've been dreaming of all my life. And by the way, I also have a secret fear that since I am getting older, if I let this relationship go, maybe no one will ever love me, and I'll die alone. I am coming to you for therapy so you can help me accept the reality of this relationship exactly as it is, without interpretation, without wishful thinking, so that I'll be in a better position to make a clear decision about whether or not I really want to stay in this relationship, to continue to work on it, or to let it go and deal with all the grief I will feel."

When we let go of our struggles with our present-moment experiences, even if they are painful, we can use that energy to consciously build a life worth living.

ACCEPTANCE OF OUR OWN EMOTIONS

Just as most of us are taught to battle our own emotions, we can learn to be kind to ourselves. While it is a bit of a cliché, it has been said that all of psychotherapy is about learning to become your own ideal parent. The ideal parent provides a "holding environment" (Winnicott, 1964) where the child can have whatever feelings they are having, though parents put boundaries on behavior.

Once when my youngest daughter was about three years old, she went to a birthday party for one of her preschool friends at a local kids' party zone. After watching the birthday girl get a large pile of presents, each of the guests received a goodie bag with a small toy inside. When my daughter opened up her bag, she discovered that she got a pink toy, and was disappointed that she did not get a purple toy, which is her favorite color. Right in the middle of the kids' party zone, my daughter began sobbing hysterically. I sat her down in my lap and told her that getting a pink toy instead of a purple one was not really a "big cry" kind of thing. Through her tears, she muttered, "I know! I don't know why I'm crying! I can't help it!" I hugged her and told her that she could cry all she wanted, but that unfortunately we had to take the pink toy and head home.

Even as adults, we often still have social pressure to "control" our emotions. My wife is a psychologist who works mostly with kids on the autism spectrum. She once described to me a team intervention with which she was involved. It was beautiful, heartfelt work, and a little boy who rarely ever connected with anyone expressed a profound interpersonal insight and made a gesture of caring, giving her a hug at the end. A little tear came down my wife's face, and the client noticed it with a smile. Afterward, the treatment team said, "We think you're becoming too emotionally attached to this child."

Now, if she had acted impulsively with that emotion, hastily swooping him up and taking him home for adoption, then that might have been a problem. But in that moment, she had a real, genuine feeling, which was a way of modeling emotional connection for the client. Acting sterile and robotic, especially when trying to teach interpersonal skills, would not have been very therapeutic. Again, feelings themselves are not things we have to get rid of, even the so-called unpleasant ones.

Our feelings give us information. They are a part of us, not outside enemies who have invaded our bodies and minds. They are messengers, and life would be bland, and even dangerous, without them. Yet people don't like those unpleasant feelings, so they tend to fight them and try to avoid them, or they avoid external circumstances that might evoke those feelings. Of course, that is not always a bad thing, because our emotions may tell us it is not safe to do certain things, and that certain people or situations could harm us. But if you are avoiding something that is important to you, your life will become restricted. We can ask clients, "Are you willing to have this anxiety, or to be uncomfortable, in order to make your life more fulfilling? Rather than avoiding or controlling the feelings, would you be willing to bring them with you on the road of life?" The control and avoidance agenda that clients tend to have actually creates more struggle.

One of the goals of ACT is to undermine the control agenda. The client comes into your office and wants you to take away their anxious feelings or distressing thoughts. What we can help them see is that their attempts to control their thoughts and feelings is often the very thing that makes the struggle ongoing. It's been said, "If you're not willing to have it, you've got it." If you don't want to think something, you're going to be thinking it. If you don't want to have anxiety, you're probably going to be anxious about getting it.

Tip for Clinicians _____

Here is a subtle thing to watch out for: Sometimes clients will use acceptance to avoid. "I'm accepting my anxiety, why doesn't it go away now?" If you are only accepting it to make it go away, you are not really accepting it. ACT's question is: "Are you willing to have it exactly as it is, whether or not it changes, in the service of something really important to you?"

As funny as it may sound at first, we can help clients befriend their anxiety and other emotions. When anxiety shows up, they can become more willing to let it be what it is, even if they don't like it. I had a client once who said, "I just kind of sit down with my anxiety like I am sitting down with a cup of coffee." That's kind of a neat way to say, "Well hello there, anxiety, my old friend!" I don't have to battle with it, and I don't have to get lost in it. It's just here right now as my companion. Then I decide what, if anything, I want to do in this moment to move me toward my values.

Through practicing acceptance, you become kinder to yourself. You begin to let go of the struggle. After all, they are *your* thoughts, feelings, and sensations. How can you win against yourself? As a metaphor for clients giving themselves complete acceptance of their anxiety, we can talk about how they might relate to a crying baby, which is the subject of the next handout.

Cradling Your Anxiety Like a Baby

If you struggle with anxiety, it can feel like you are in a constant battle for your life. However, since your anxiety is coming from your own body and your own mind, fighting yourself only leads to long-term exhaustion. While the experience of anxiety can be very unpleasant to say the least, **instead of fighting yourself, you can learn to give yourself compassion.**

I once worked with a woman named Betty, who had the worst case of anxiety I had ever seen. She was so anxious that she literally could not stop shaking all over, all day long. Her husband had to drive her to the appointment, and I noticed the shaking when I met them in the waiting room. Betty paced back and forth in my office for most of the appointment. My first thought was that she had a neurological disorder, like Parkinson's Disease.

Betty's husband sat down and explained to me that she had received all kinds of medical tests, such as blood tests, heart tests, and brain scans, and they could find nothing wrong with her physically. They said she just had anxiety. **Yet, everything she tried to do to get rid of the anxiety, like relaxation techniques and antianxiety medications, only seemed to make things worse.**

When I asked Betty what was important in her life, she said being a mother was near the top of the list. She had a daughter, who was now grown up, and was about to have her first baby. This woman was thrilled at the thought of becoming a grandmother. However, the daughter said, "If you don't get this anxiety under control, there is no way I'm letting you anywhere near my baby!" **This of course made her anxious about being anxious.**

I told her that while there might be something deeper going on, what I could see right away was that she was fighting her own anxiety. And I said, "Of course you're fighting it! This anxiety is very intense, and it probably feels like it has been ripping your life apart, so it's very understandable that you don't want to feel it! But this anxiety is your own body, doing what it is designed to do. It's doing it a lot more than you want it to right now, but this is not an alien invader. Your own body and feelings are not your enemies."

An analogy that she found helpful was to think of her anxiety as a crying baby. "If a baby is screaming and crying, you don't yell and scream back at the baby—that only makes them more upset. Assuming it's not a pinched diaper or something, all you can do is cradle the baby gently in your arms and rock them quietly, just letting the baby cry."

Betty seemed intrigued, and I continued. "You can do the same thing with your own emotions. The feelings belong to you, after all. There is no need to struggle with yourself. Show yourself some kindness when your anxiety is overwhelming." I asked Betty to sit down for a moment, which she was willing to do. "As funny as this may sound, just place your hands on your own body, maybe one on your heart and the other on your belly. Treat the anxiety like a crying baby, feeling full of love for this baby even if they are crying. Just stay present with it as best you can, even if nothing changes."

Betty actually stopped shaking for the first time in weeks. While just doing that once did not fix everything, it was a big step in learning to relate differently to her anxiety.

You can practice this for yourself as well. When you are feeling anxious, find a quiet place you can just sit with it. Hold it like you would a crying baby, or like you are giving a hug to a friend in distress. It may get worse, or it may go away, but just practice letting it do what it needs to do. If you've been practicing fighting your emotions all your life, it may take some time to develop the ability to be kind to yourself. Even doing this for a few minutes a day can start to break old, unhelpful habits.

Give yourself permission to feel, even if you don't like those feelings. Sometimes you need to cry like a baby. When you do, you can give yourself compassion. Life throws enough challenges our way, so we don't need to add to our distress by fighting with ourselves.

Tip for Clinicians _____

Remember that ACT is about being more flexible, not fighting your own emotions. We can accidently get hooked into trying to fix or take away our clients' anxiety. Since we are all trained to help people feel better, we can inadvertently reinforce this struggle by trying to get rid of their feelings. While relaxation or distraction can be good for long-term self-care, if you use it to get rid of anxiety, you could be reinforcing avoidance. We can model presence and curiosity by asking things like "It looks like you're really anxious right now. Where do you feel that in your body? Is this an old feeling?" We can also model acceptance with appropriate self-disclosure, like "I'm feeling a little anxious right now too, but I'm okay with it being here, and I'm willing to stay with this if you are."

The following exercise is called "physicalizing" (Hayes, 2007; Hayes, Strosahl, & Wilson, 2012), and is similar to the exercise done with thoughts in the chapter on defusion. Putting the anxiety out in front of the client, and imagining what physical attributes it might have, helps them to step back and get some perspective on it. While it may be best to read this to the client the first time they do it so they can focus on the process, clients can do this on their own to practice it at home.

Getting Perspective on Your Anxiety

Everyone experiences anxiety. It is a natural part of being alive, at least if you're paying attention. It helps motivate you to take action when something important is happening or when something needs to be done.

But since anxiety is unpleasant, we often develop ways of trying to get rid of it, to ignore it, to push it away. Unfortunately, this can often lead the anxiety to grow bigger and bigger in our minds over time. This makes us even more reluctant to be with it, and we try harder and harder to keep it out of our minds.

It's a little like noticing a shadow on the wall that looks like a tiger is creeping up behind you. You don't want to turn and look, because you think you won't like what you see. Your fear grows and grows as the shadow gets larger.

But if you turn around, it may well be a small kitten projecting that big shadow. **If you turn and investigate the anxiety, it may not always be what your mind has made it out to be.**

Whatever it might be, it is usually better to look right at it than to stick your head in the sand and hope it goes away. Ignoring your anxiety has probably not been working for you, at least not more than temporarily. It is important to get to know this anxiety, since you may well have given control of your life over to it. In this exercise, we are going to practice stepping back from the anxiety to get a broader perspective on it.

As you sit with the questions below, your logical, thinking mind might think this is weird, or corny. You may wonder how this could possibly help. It's the mind's job to protect you, so if that happens, thank your mind and go back to doing the exercise as best you can. If you want things to be different in your life, you need to be willing to do something different.

Ideally, find a quiet, comfortable place where you won't be interrupted. Notice what your mind does as you settle into the place you are—it will likely keep trying to distract you. That's okay—it's just trying to help again. Notice where your mind goes and practice bringing your attention back to the exercise.

Imagine that your anxiety takes physical form and is floating in the air about 10 feet out in front of you.

If it had a size, how big would your anxiety be?

_____

131

If it had a shape, what shape would your anxiety be?

_____

If it had a color, what color would your anxiety be?

_____

If it had a speed, how fast would your anxiety be moving?

_____

If it had a smell, what would your anxiety smell like?

_____

If it had a weight, how heavy would your anxiety be?

_____

If it had a level of power, how much power would it have to push you around?

_____

Continue to observe this vision of the anxiety out in front you for a few minutes. If you find this challenging, just do the best you can. As you watch it, ask yourself the following questions.

How much power, time, and energy have you been giving to this anxiety?

_____

_____

_____

As you look at this anxiety, seeing its shape, color, size, and speed, is it really something that is going to destroy you? Is this something that demands you constantly fight with it? Does it really need you to spend so much of your time and energy pushing it away?

_____

_____

Is this thing worth giving up your life for? Do you really want to give up on your values for this thing?

_____

_____

If it meant that you could live a more fulfilling life, whatever that means to you, would you be willing to allow this thing to be exactly as it is? Of course you don't like it, but would you be willing to allow it to be your companion if it meant you could do more of the things that matter to you?

_____

_____

Pay close attention to what your mind does with this next question:

Are you willing to take that anxiety back now? To be with it and hold it, even if you don't like it? In some ways, this old companion of yours has tried to help you, to protect you. Could you imagine embracing it as if it were a child or friend that you love, even if they were covered in mud and smelly? Or, would you be willing to imagine shrinking or folding up that anxiety, and sticking it in your pocket? Not as something you are, but as something you can carry with you?

_____

_____

If the answer to the above question is yes, just spend a few more minutes with this anxiety, this old, familiar companion of yours.

If the answer to the above question is no, continue with the next questions.

Get in touch with the resistance, fear, and/or hesitancy to take this anxiety back. Imagine moving your visualization of the anxiety off to one side, then imagine this resistance out in front of you.

If it had a size, how big would your resistance be?

_____

If it had a shape, what shape would your resistance be?

_____

If it had a color, what color would your resistance be?

_____

If it had a speed, how fast would your resistance be moving?

_____

If it had a smell, what would your resistance smell like?

_____

If it had a weight, how heavy would your resistance be?

_____

If it had a level of power, how much power would it have to push you around?

_____

As you look at this resistance, seeing its shape, color, size, and speed, is it really something that is going to destroy you? Is this something that demands you constantly fight with it? Do you really need to spend time and energy trying to push it away?

_____

_____

Is this thing worth giving up your life for? Do you really want to give up on your values for this thing?

_____

_____

If it meant that you could live a more fulfilling life, whatever that means to you, would you be willing to allow this thing to be exactly as it is? Of course you don't like it, but would you be willing to allow it to be your companion if it meant you could do more of the things that matter to you?

_____

_____

Again, pay close attention to what your mind does with this next question:

Are you willing to take that resistance back now? To be with it and hold it, even if you don't like it? In some ways, this old companion of yours has tried to help you, to protect you. Could you imagine embracing it as if it were a child or friend that you love, even if they were covered in mud and smelly? Or, would you be willing to imagine shrinking or folding up that resistance, and sticking it in your pocket? Not as something you are, but as something you can carry with you?

_____

If the answer to the above question is no, then repeat the exercise about taking back the resistance. If the answer is yes, then go back to the question about taking back the anxiety.

You have probably spent many years ignoring, battling, or pushing away your anxiety, so be patient with yourself as you practice this exercise. Consider this exercise as an experiment in doing things differently, and see if you can suspend your expectations and judgments about whether or not you are doing it "right."

ACCEPTANCE AND TRAUMA

Trauma is a very common issue in clinical work. For clients who have experienced trauma, there are some special considerations, but the principles of avoidance and acceptance are especially important here. A big factor in the perpetuation of PTSD is the battle that goes on between thoughts, memories, feelings, and body sensations. Because these things are so uncomfortable, the trauma survivor just doesn't want to have those distressing experiences. They try to set up their lives in such a way that they don't experience things that might remind them of the trauma, and end up living a more and more restricted life. Because it becomes so restricted, their experience of life becomes all about survival, not living.

Since PTSD is perpetuated by avoidance, not surprisingly, if mindfulness-based approaches are used to distract clients with PTSD from their symptoms, they can become worse (Boeschen, Koss, Figuerdo, & Coan, 2001; Sears & Chard, 2016). However, using mindfulness and acceptance can help clients become more comfortable with their discomfort. In other words, they become less afraid of the unpleasant experiences that come up. When they are less afraid of their internal experiences, they are more willing to go out and do the things that are important to them. In other words, they become more flexible.

Here's a personal example of how I helped my daughter through a traumatic experience. Last Christmas Day, it was 60 degrees Fahrenheit outside, but there was still a thick layer of ice on our one-acre pond. In a lapse of judgment on my part, I thought it would be a great idea to take my 10-year-old daughter out on the canoe. I put a little electric motor on the back, and we used it to build up speed and ram into the ice. It was fun to watch it crack. After a while, we were able to break a path into the middle of the pond.

At one point, I aimed the motor 90 degrees to the canoe, and tried to put it in reverse to back out of a place where we had gotten stuck. My hand slipped, and it went into full power, causing the boat to lurch. My daughter and I lost our balance and fell against the opposite side of the boat. As the boat tipped, the edge went below the water line. The canoe immediately filled with water and completely flipped over, throwing us into the water.

I don't remember all of the details of what happened in those few seconds. I do clearly remember my face slamming into the ice and feeling the brutal cold on my body as I went under. Luckily, my daughter always wears a life jacket, but I only had a seat cushion float. I had just finished using the chainsaw for about an hour, so my exhausted muscles were very weak in the freezing water.

When my head popped up out of the water, I could not see my daughter. I realized that she must have gotten trapped under the canoe, with her life jacket pushing her up into it. As I moved closer, I was hoping that air was trapped under the canoe so she could breathe, but when I got myself under it, there was only a tiny amount of air, not enough to breathe. Sure enough, my daughter's life jacket was pushing her up into the canoe. I grabbed her jacket and yanked her down and to the side as best I could. I had no leverage, and in my shoes and coat it was hard to maneuver. I was thankful that she did not fight me in the confusion. After a few moments, I got her past the edge of the canoe, and she popped up out of the water.

Later, my daughter told me she wasn't sure what to do. She feared that even if she could get out, she might have gotten trapped under the ice. She said she had told herself she should just give up and die, just before she felt me grab her life jacket.

With the boat motor still buzzing loudly in the air, and broken ice all around us, I told my daughter we had to swim to the dock, about 50 yards away. We began yelling for my wife, and she came after a few minutes, but there was nothing she could do without putting herself in danger. I told my daughter we had to swim through the path we had made in the ice, but in Wonder Woman style, she slammed her fists into the ice to create her own more direct path. Between the cold, my exhaustion, and worrying about my daughter, it was a very long swim. In the last few yards, my wife threw a rope out to us and pulled our shivering bodies out of the water.

After we each took long hot showers, we all snuggled on the couch the rest of the day, crying and expressing our feelings and appreciation for each other.

For several days, my daughter would have random moments of fear and crying. She would tell me, "I can't stop thinking about it!"

It would have been tempting to never talk about it again, or to tell her to try not to think about it, or to distract her from the thoughts and feelings. I just kept hugging her and letting her know it was normal to have those thoughts and feelings. When she said she would never forget, I told her that was true, but eventually she would remember it without all these strong feelings. She said she would never get on the pond again. I told her she would never have to, but maybe someday she might change her mind.

About two weeks later, while we were standing at the end of our driveway waiting for the school bus one morning, my daughter told me about a dream she had the night before:

> I dreamed that we invited a bunch of friends and relatives over for a big party. Everyone had their own boat or raft, and we all went out onto the pond. As we were out on the pond, a hand came up out of the water and grabbed my ankle. It pulled me down into the water, and you just sat there and watched, and you didn't do anything!

My heart wrenched. I of course gave her a big hug and assured her that I would never let that happen. But I also normalized that dream for her, letting her know that her brain was just playing out the thing that really scared her and that eventually the dreams would go away.

In the months since, my daughter has gone from never wanting to be anywhere near the pond, to being able to sit by it, to thinking that when it is warmer she will want to go out on a raft (something that she can push off her head, she told me).

Breaking the Avoidance Cycle

PTSD represents an extreme in battling with our emotions and thoughts. The clients don't want to have those memories, and they don't want to have those feeling in their bodies, so they continuously try to ignore them, fight them, or control them. Basically, the cortex of the brain, where thinking takes place, is saying, "That was an awful memory! I don't want to remember that!" No human being would want to remember a traumatic event. But the limbic system, which fires up the emotions, keeps saying, "You almost died! You witnessed something horrifying! You've got to learn from this! You can't forget this! It could save your life in the future!" Hence, there is a constant battle between the cortex (thinking) and the limbic system (feeling), which bursts out as reexperiencing symptoms—flashbacks, nightmares, and intrusive thoughts, feelings, and memories.

To break this struggle, clients can learn to practice acceptance of the emotions and thoughts. They can develop the attitude of just noticing, "Here comes that image again of what happened to me. Here comes that fear feeling." They can learn to have compassion for these thoughts and emotions, rather than trying to fight to get rid of them. This is a very powerful ingredient in the treatment of trauma.

If something is triggered in the client during a session, it is important not to immediately try to get rid of the thoughts and feelings. We don't want to get caught up in fighting with their internal experiences. We can simply say, "Sounds like you are having a strong reaction right now. I know you've had a lot of these before. What are you noticing right now?" **In this way, we are modeling how to stay present with these uncomfortable reactions.**

Of course, like any specialty area of psychotherapy, you want to make sure you get good training in working with trauma. I was giving a workshop at a national conference years ago, and an audience member asked, "You just said you wrote a book on mindfulness and PTSD. Wouldn't mindfulness make trauma worse?" I replied, "Yes, it can, especially in the beginning, because now you are paying more attention to what's there, and they've spent years practicing avoidance." The man replied, "Well, I have a client with PTSD that I'm working with right now, and whenever we start talking about anything remotely related to the trauma, she gets upset, so we change the subject." Do you see how in that case, **the client pulled the therapist into the avoidance cycle too?**

At the other extreme, clients can be thrust into their experiences much too quickly. When I was working at the VA Medical Center, I once heard a concerning story from a Vietnam veteran. A couple of years before, he had been working with a therapist (and I can't imagine this person was licensed) who thought it would be a great idea to do a psychodramatic reenactment of the client's time in Vietnam. The therapist acted like the sergeant, and they acted out a past event the client had talked about. Not surprisingly, the client flashed back and started choking the therapist. That was obviously a bad idea.

Interestingly, newer research has shown that **it is not even necessary to get into the nitty gritty details of the actual traumatic events** (Resick, Monson, & Chard, 2016). Trauma survivors can grow by learning different ways of relating to the automatic thoughts and emotional reactions that got stuck because of the trauma.

Posttraumatic Growth

Around 70 percent of people experience a significant trauma at some point in their lives, and have symptoms for a little while (Cromer & Smyth, 2010). However, only about 7 percent actually get PTSD, where the clinically significant and life-interfering symptoms continue for at least a month or longer (Kessler et al., 2005).

What makes the difference between those who recover and those who develop lasting PTSD? There are a lot of different factors, but a big piece is that when you are caught up in fighting, battling, and avoiding, you end up living a very restricted life. At that point, your values become less important to you, and a major part of your life becomes avoidance and struggle. Of course, be careful how you express this to clients. It's not their fault that they get stuck in their past. It's certainly not their fault that horrendous things happened to them. But if the events did happen, we want to help them build a life worth living from this point forward.

Interestingly, there has been recent research on resilience and posttraumatic growth, which involves how the mind makes meaning from the event (Calhoun & Tedeschi, 2014). Some people go through trauma and actually get stronger.

Of course, be very careful about how you talk about this with clients. I would never tell a client, especially in the beginning, "Hey, you're going to be a better person because of this awful trauma!" In fact, I've personally had people tell me that in the past when I was going through some really terrible experiences. At the time, I was angry when I heard that. But now, years later, I can look back and realize that I would not be the psychologist I am today if I had not gone through those experiences. I wouldn't wish them on anybody else, and I'm not sure I would want to experience those things again if given the chance, but I did learn and grow a lot.

Alternatively, I could have ended up getting stuck in those experiences. I could have ruminated on thoughts like "It's not fair. This should never have happened. It was other people's fault. They did this to me!" I could have easily stayed stuck in that thinking the rest of my life, and guess what—the thinking was factually accurate—they shouldn't have done that to me. However, by accepting the reality of what happened, and that I can't change the past, I gained the freedom to choose in the present moment. **The important question is: "What kind of life do I want to make now with the time that I do have?"**

It can be helpful to validate a client's experiences, and to talk about how their reactions have been helpful in the past, before shifting to how they can learn from them. I was once working with a combat veteran who had recently returned from Afghanistan. One day, as we were sitting in the office, he said, "You know, people don't have any idea. Underneath that curtain there, there could be an IED (Improvised Explosive Device). There could be a bomb in that trash can over there. We don't know what's in that water bottle. Someone could be hiding behind those closet doors. This is a drop ceiling— there could be anything up there."

I calmly said, "You know what? I bet your ability to notice these things saved your life in Afghanistan. I bet you had buddies who died because they didn't notice the things that you're able to notice. That noticing kept you alive. Noticing is not a bad thing. You're absolutely right, a lot of stuff could happen right now, and most people would be caught totally off guard."

He seemed to relax as he felt heard, and I continued. "It seems like the real problem is not the noticing, it is what happens after you notice. It sounds like you get caught up in your thoughts about what you notice, and you get caught up in your emotions. You try hard not to notice things, but you can't help it. Then you fight yourself, trying not to notice what you notice."

He nodded in agreement, and I went on. "From what you told me, because of all of this, you have stopped doing the things that are important to you, and you end up staying home most of the time. What we can work on in here is the ability to notice without getting caught up in ruminating about noticing. It may not be easy at first, but you can learn to just be aware of the feelings that come up when you notice potential danger, and then ask yourself, 'Do I want to go out anyway to be with my family? Do I want to go to this event, even though I know that I might be anxious?' You might not believe me right now, but all that training in noticing may end up being a good thing in the future. It will make you a better employee at work, and it will help to keep your family safe."

Through learning acceptance, clients can begin to relate differently to their experiences. Trying to talk someone out of their thoughts and feelings may end up reinforcing avoidance. Clients can practice noticing their experiences without getting lost or caught up in them.

Responding Skillfully to Clients

Therapists often worry about what to do if a client starts having a trauma reaction in the therapy session. Again, our responses to the client's reactions help to model an attitude of resilience and growth.

Some therapists fear that if they work with trauma, the client is going to explode with emotions. Of course, clients' emotions and thoughts can seem stronger when they open up to them, because they have been working hard to push them down or ignore them. Whatever happens, we can model for clients that if the emotions and thoughts are already here anyway, we can practice noticing them as they are, even if they are uncomfortable.

As discussed in the last chapter, we can also shift from content to process to modulate any trauma reaction. If a client starts having a trauma reaction in session, we can shift to the processes they are experiencing. "How fast is your heart beating right now?" or "What are you noticing in your stomach?" or "What thoughts are coming up for you right now?"

Though rare, if somebody starts having a flashback, and dissociates, you can re-engage the frontal lobes of the brain by calmly grounding them in the present moment. "Okay, what I would like you to do now is open your eyes and look at the floor and tell me what color the carpet is."

Memory Reconsolidation

Interestingly, there is some newer research that supports our clinical experience in working with trauma. It's called memory reconsolidation (Alberini & LeDoux, 2013; Nader & Einarsson, 2010). When your memories are retrieved, for a moment they are fluid and changeable before they are reconsolidated in the brain.

Human memories are not like computer files. Ostensibly, when you save something on a computer, it is stored digitally in a specific place on the memory drive. When you pull it back up, it is exactly the same as it was before.

However, in the human brain, memories are spread out in a variety of places. If you find this moment memorable later on, the visual memories are going to be stored in the visual cortex, and the auditory memories in the temporal lobes. You'll have a certain feeling state associated with this moment stored somewhere in the limbic system. The words you are reading right now will likely be stored in the left hemisphere of the cortex.

This is a bit of an oversimplification, but basically, the hippocampus is like a key. It keeps track of where all the memories are stored. When you remember something, the hippocampus pulls the different types of memories back together from all those different places in the brain. Human memory is a reconstructive process.

During trauma, the hippocampus can get disrupted, so basically the key becomes lost. Memories are there in different parts of the brain, but they are no longer organized. And of course, with traumatic memories, you don't want to remember the events, so they are basically kept stuck.

However, when a memory does come up, there is a moment it becomes fluid. **There is an opportunity to associate a new feeling state with that memory before it is reconsolidated.** If you alter that memory while you are remembering it, now you can lay it back down a little bit differently than it was last stored.

File Cabinet Technique

We can take advantage of the memory reconsolidation process, and also teach the principles of acceptance, with a technique called "file cabinet" (Hayes, 2007). When a strong feeling comes up for a client, we can look at a variety of things this feeling is associated with, as if thumbing through a filing cabinet. We can inquire about other images and memories related to that feeling. This gives us a broader perspective on and acceptance of the feeling. The feeling itself is not our enemy when we look at it in context. It is also often a way to become more flexible with the feeling states associated with those memories.

I once worked with a woman named Joan. One day, she came in saying, "All week long, I just couldn't get rid of this feeling of being angry. I can't stop thinking that people are stupid and cruel; that no one cares about other people's feelings."

"Are those feelings here now?" I asked.

"Yes. They're pretty strong."

"Well, as long as they're here anyway, let's invite them into the room," I suggested. "Where do you feel those feelings in your body?"

Joan was quickly able to notice. "There's a tightness in my chest, and it feels like there is a lead ball in my gut." I invited her to just sit with the feeling. Very often, letting go of the battle with a feeling tends to soften it, but as we talked, I got a sense that there was more going on here, so I asked a simple question. "Is this a new feeling, or an old feeling? Is it a feeling you've had before?"

"Definitely an old feeling."

"If you're willing, let's try something different," I said, and Joan nodded in agreement. "With this feeling here now, I want you to move through any past pictures in your mind associated with this feeling, as if you could skim through a file cabinet. In fact, see if you can get in touch with one of the oldest memories associated with this feeling. It doesn't have to be the perfect memory, but can you remember one of the first times you felt this way?"

Almost immediately, perhaps because of the concept of mood-state dependent learning and memory, she was able to recall a scene from the ninth grade. She had stayed late at the high school working on a project. By the time she left, all the teachers and adults had gone home. When she walked out the front door, she looked across the parking lot, and saw four teenaged boys at the flagpole with a live cat. She watched in horror as they put the cat up the flagpole. She felt completely helpless, because she knew it would not be wise to confront four boys, and there were no adults around.

She told me later that she had not remembered that scene since it had happened. No wonder she had all those angry feelings and thoughts about people being stupid and cruel!

I next asked her to imagine that she could somehow magically freeze that scene and go back in time to that ninth-grade self. "What would you do, or say, or give to that ninth-grade self that she never got back then?" She gave herself a hug, expressed empathy for her feelings, and let her know that it wasn't her fault.

I next asked her, "What do you think that ninth-grade self would want to say to the you of today?" After sitting quietly for a few moments, she said, "That you don't have to be angry at everybody in your life just because four boys did a terrible thing."

Of course, she will never forget that memory, and I will never forget that memory, and now perhaps you will never forget that memory. But after doing this exercise, that memory feels different to her. She has learned to have that memory without fighting it, and without it affecting her current life decisions as much.

As a side note, it can be helpful to have the client do this exercise with a much younger self if possible. It tends to be easier to give our young selves more compassion than our current selves. Notice too that it is not necessary to get into the nitty gritty details of the trauma. Just relating differently to the feelings that come up can be helpful.

You can see that all of the ACT processes—values, mindfulness, self-as-context, acceptance, defusion, and committed action—can come out in an exercise like this. It also shares aspects with the "empty chair" technique from Gestalt therapy.

Use the following worksheet to guide your clients through this exercise. I highly recommend you do this in session with them several times before suggesting they try it on their own. I also recommend watching a live demonstration of this technique by Dr. Joanne Dahl in the video series ACT in Action, available at NewHarbinger.com (Hayes, 2007).

File Cabinet Exercise

Sometimes old feelings like anxiety can become stuck in our brains. Our current emotions can become magnified by past events. **While we may never forget the unpleasant things that have happened to us, we can change the way our brains relate to them.** One way to do this is through a technique called "file cabinet," where we flip through the files in our minds to get a different perspective on our thoughts and feelings.

I once worked with a man named Larry who wanted help with his relationship. He said he'd been married over 20 years, and overall things were good. However, he told me, "I keep doing this weird thing—I'm so afraid of conflict that I will make up little white lies about things. Even for small things, I don't want to upset my wife, so I just say a white lie, and then I have to remember that white lie. That leads to another one, then to another one. When she discovers the lie, it's really embarrassing. She doesn't even get that mad when she finds out. She just feels hurt, and doesn't understand why I do it. I don't even understand why I do it. I know it's silly. I should just say the truth even if it is a little uncomfortable."

I told Larry, "You know, I bet you have thought about this a lot. Since you're a therapist yourself, you've probably tried to figure it out intellectually, and have told yourself to just stop it, but you keep doing it anyway. Would you be willing to do something different to get a different outcome?"

Larry eagerly agreed. "Absolutely! That's why I'm here!"

I first had Larry get in touch with that feeling. "I want you to bring to mind how you feel when you start telling these white lies to your wife. Notice how that feels, and where it comes up in your body. Have you felt this feeling before? Can you recall a time, perhaps in your childhood, when you felt this same feeling?"

An image immediately came into Larry's mind. "I'm remembering when I was about six years old, and I was in a van with my parents. My parents were in the front seat, and they were yelling and screaming, and they were slapping each other back and forth. I had this feeling like I've got to fix this. What can I do? How do I stop this?"

Since that was probably a regular experience in Larry's childhood, no wonder he didn't like conflict! To help him relate differently to the feeling connected to this memory, I said, "Imagine you could magically freeze-frame that moment in time, and maybe even remove your parents from the scene. Imagine that the you of today could magically travel back in time to that six-year-old boy. What do you think that six-year-old boy needed that no one else gave him back then?"

Larry burst into tears. "I would give him a hug, and tell him, 'You're okay just as you are. You're not doing anything wrong. It's not your fault that your parents are arguing.'"

After he sat with the feelings for a moment, I asked him, "What do you think that six-year-old boy would say to the you of today?"

Larry smiled. "He would probably say, 'Wow, you're pretty cool! You have a great job and a great wife! You don't have to lie to her. You're not going to get in trouble.'"

While this one session did not fix everything for Larry, it created a shift in the way he related to his feelings. He began to heal and let go of old patterns. **While he never forgot his traumatic memories, they began to have less power over him.**

When you have strong feelings of your own coming up, you can try this exercise for yourself. The first few times you do it, you should have a licensed psychotherapist help you through the process.

Begin the exercise in a quiet place where you will not be interrupted. Allow yourself to get in touch with the feelings that are here right now. It may be challenging to put into words, but how would you describe this feeling? Where do you feel this in your physical body? What physical sensations are you noticing?

_____

_____

_____

_____

_____

_____

Once the feeling is clearly here, imagine that you could open the drawer of a file cabinet where you store your memories related to this particular feeling. What images or memories come to mind? You may have recent memories, or you may have old memories. Make a list of what comes up.

_____

_____

_____

_____

_____

Now, pick one of the memories to work with. Freeze-frame the scene in your mind and describe the general situation.

_____

_____

_____

_____

_____

Next, imagine you can somehow magically go back in time to that scene. What did that younger self need that you did not get at the time? What would you want to do, or give, or say to that younger self? Take a moment to imagine what it would have been like to receive what you needed at that young age.

_____

_____

_____

_____

_____

Next, imagine what that younger self would want to tell the you of today. Would your younger self want to give you anything? It could be advice, a hug, or just a smile. Just see what comes to mind.

_____

_____

_____

_____

_____

_____

Whenever you are ready, bring this exercise to a close and return your attention to the room you are in. Notice your surroundings. What do you see and hear? What are you feeling?

Part of this exercise is to give yourself permission to have your own feelings, which perhaps you were not allowed to do in the past. Spend a few moments just allowing yourself to feel, even if those feelings are not very pleasant.

As with the example above, doing this exercise once may not make much difference, but over time, you can learn to let go of the struggle with your own experiences. You are teaching yourself that it is okay to be you.

INCREASING SELF-COMPASSION

When clients learn acceptance of their own experiences, it results in increased self-compassion. When they learn to notice their thoughts, emotions, and body sensations, without beating themselves up for having them, they end up being kinder to themselves.

For clients who have an ingrained habit of fighting their own experiences, we can artificially create a sense of acceptance, not to avoid other feelings, but to get a taste of what self-compassion might feel like (Neff & Tirch, 2013). You can use the following exercise for ideas about how to do this, or you might choose to read this script to guide a client through the exercise. You can also give this to a client to practice on their own. Of course, it can be very helpful to therapists as well. You or the client can make an audio recording of this exercise or use the free recording on my website: www.psych-insights.com. For more on ACT and the science of compassion, see Tirch, Schoendorff, and Silberstein (2014).

Generating Acceptance and Compassion for Self and Others

When you struggle for years with strong emotions like anxiety, it can be easy to lose touch with feeling compassion and acceptance for yourself and others. This exercise is something you can practice in order to get back in touch with these feelings.

Find a quiet place to sit or lie down. Settle into a comfortable position, whatever that means for you. You might choose to close your eyes, or you can just shade them and look down in front of you.

Begin by bringing to mind someone or something that for you represents the ideal embodiment of acceptance, compassion, and love, and imagine this floating above you in the sky. It could be a divine being. It could be a person that you admire, living or dead. It could be a historical figure, a fictional character, or someone you know. It could be an animal. It could even just be a symbol. Find something or someone that represents for you that feeling of being accepted and loved, or what for you would be the embodiment of pure compassion. See what comes to mind, and then visualize that floating in the sky a little bit in front of you and a little above you.

Next, imagine that this being, or this symbol, is just so overflowing with compassion that it emanates out and enters into your body. You can imagine this in different ways. You can imagine that it is a beam of light or love that flows into your head and then down into your body, or you can imagine the person or symbol just embracing you fully and filling you with these feelings of love, acceptance, and compassion. See if you can imagine receiving this ultimate compassion, this unconditional acceptance, into your own body. Imagine that the entire universe is being channeled through this symbol or this being and flows into you. Visualize this energy first filling up your heart, then spilling out and filling up your entire body.

You don't have to do anything to deserve this. You don't have to feel like you've earned it. All you have to do is receive it. See if you can allow it to fill you up. You don't even have to feel it or believe it, just imagine what it would feel like to receive this unconditional acceptance, this love, this compassion. Imagine it filling up your entire body.

Next, bring to mind someone you really care about, someone to whom you would like to send some of this love, some of this compassion, some of this acceptance. You might imagine them in front of and a little below you. See this compassion and acceptance coming in from this being or this symbol into you, filling you up, then flowing out into this person that you really care about. Imagine all this energy and caring flowing into them.

This process doesn't take any energy away from you. You're not used up in this process. It's like there's an infinite supply of this compassion throughout the universe, and it's just being channeled through this being or symbol, into you, and into this person that you care about. Picture yourself as a conduit through which all this energy flows, without any effort on your part.

You might choose to stay with the same person for a while, or you might choose to bring to mind other people that you care about. Send each one this compassion, this love, this total acceptance. Just allow this love to flow through you and into these loved ones.

Next, bring to mind some individuals toward whom you don't necessarily have good or bad feelings, and send each of them this compassion, this acceptance, this love. They could be people you noticed out in public in the last few days. They could be co-workers or casual acquaintances. You may or may not have any particular feelings about them. They are fellow human beings. Continue to practice the same thing, allowing this acceptance and compassion to flow through you and into these people that you don't necessarily know very well. You know that they would appreciate receiving this. See what faces appear in your mind, and send this energy along to each one of them.

Of course, you can't control whether or not they receive this compassion or acceptance. Just send it along to them. You're not forcing it on them. Just allow it to flow through you and into them.

Next, bring to mind some people that you don't really like very much, that you find irritating, or that bother you. If this is one of the first times you are doing this exercise, it probably isn't a good idea to bring up the worst offender, or the person you hate the most in life. In the beginning, just practice with somebody that you find a little irritating or bothersome. Imagine that they are out in front of you, and do the same thing you did before. Allow this energy to flow in from this being or this symbol into you, through you, and into this person that you don't like very much. Send this compassion, this sense of acceptance along to them.

Now, sending compassion and acceptance to these individuals doesn't necessarily mean that you like these people now, or that you are okay with the things that they have done in the past, or that you approve of the things that they continue to do. It doesn't mean that you won't keep setting boundaries, or that you will no longer keep them out of your life if you have chosen to do that. You do not have to accept their behaviors, but you can send the person acceptance. No matter how irritating they may be, somewhere inside them is a human being that wants to be happy.

If you are really having trouble with this, you might imagine the person as a little baby. Chances are, when they were born, they were not pure evil. It may be deep inside, but there is a part of them that is a human being that wants love and acceptance. Just imagine sending that along. Again, it doesn't mean you approve of their behavior. You also can't control if they accept it or not. Just allow it to flow through you into the human being that is in front of you.

As you do this, your brain might rebel. It might tell you that you don't want to do this, that you don't like this person, or that they don't deserve this. That's okay. Can you just let the thoughts be there? There is no need to argue with them. Just keep sending the energy along.

You may even notice some uncomfortable feelings coming up, but just keep imagining this compassion flowing into these people that you don't really like very much. Again, you could continue doing this with the same person, or you could have several different people appearing in your mind. Just send each one this acceptance and compassion.

After a few minutes, let the images of all those people dissolve away. Spend a few moments just receiving this acceptance and love for yourself. Imagine this being or symbol of ultimate compassion and acceptance, in the sky above you, sending this down to you, and let yourself receive it for a few more moments. Allow it to fill your heart and to fill your body with acceptance of how you are, exactly as you are in this moment.

Maybe this sense of complete acceptance and unconditional love is a new feeling, or maybe this is an old feeling. Maybe at some point in your life, you had a friend or a relative, like a grandparent, that brought up this feeling for you. No matter what you did, you knew that they just accepted you for who you were. They may not have always liked what you did, but they accepted you for who you were. See if you can allow that feeling to come up for you right now.

Next, imagine that energy shrinking down to the size of your heart. Take a few moments to allow that feeling of accepting yourself just as you are to reside in your heart. It doesn't mean you're not going to grow or change in the future, but for right now in this moment, who you are is okay. In this moment, it doesn't matter what you have done in the past. In this moment, it is okay to be who you are, exactly as you are.

When you are ready to let this exercise go, see if you can allow this feeling to stay in your heart. Slowly bring your attention back to the rest of the room, and allow your eyes to come open if they were closed. Take a few moments to absorb this experience before you go back to your daily activities.

After the exercise, take some time to reflect on your experience. Do this practice on a regular basis for a few weeks, and take note of the different experiences you have. Just as with physical exercise, it takes time and practice to develop and strengthen one's capacity for compassion.

Processing the Exercise

There are a lot of different variations of the previous exercise, so feel free to experiment on what works best for different clients (and for yourself).

As with other exercises, processing clients' experiences afterward can open more insights. Some people have trouble sending compassion to people they dislike. It's like they want world peace, but not for *that* person! Some people have an insight that their angry reactions toward certain people make them look worse than the person causing the problems in their lives.

Clients can also realize that holding onto anger toward others just eats away at themselves. Sometimes I practice this exercise on a certain relative of mine. This person has been through some serious life problems, and has caused my family a lot of grief. But right now, he is doing better than he ever has in his life. He is doing all the right things, and is finally making visible changes, and not just talking about it. Yet, I still sometimes have that automatic reaction of "Look at all those awful things you did to me in the past!" If I didn't notice that reaction, it could interfere with my ability to support the good stuff he is doing. Of course, I won't forget what happened, but walking around with that anger is not going to change him in any way. I would only be harming myself.

Of course, I can imagine sending compassion and still set clear boundaries. I will never loan money to that relative (again). I simply stopped carrying the anger and the hatred inside myself. I can even give myself permission to not like the feelings I'm having, and just practice staying present with them. Strong feelings may motivate us to do something, like write a letter, go on a protest march, or speak up about an injustice, but holding onto anger only eats away at ourselves.

Sometimes compassion can look terrifying. Remember when you were a kid, and a parent, teacher, or other adult cared enough about you to set boundaries or tell you something that was hard for you to hear? That is fierce compassion. That takes courage. They weren't doing it out of anger, or because they had a chip on their shoulder. They were doing it because it is what you needed, though at the time you might have thought they were being mean.

A small child might say, "I want a candy bar!" If I say no, they think I'm being mean, but that is compassion, because in that moment too much sugar might not be a good thing. That's why in some of the iconography of Asia, they have paintings of enlightened beings that look angry, or like a demon. They are symbolically attacking illusion, cutting through ignorance with the sword of wisdom. It is acknowledging reality whether you like it or not. Compassion doesn't mean you let people do whatever they want. We may need to take some really firm action, but it doesn't need to be an automatic reaction to anger.

This compassion exercise can be especially useful for therapists to practice. As you all know, some of our clients have done horrendous things. Before we were therapists, we might have been pretty judgmental, or just plain angry and hateful toward some of these people. Yet, here they are now, trying to get help. Somewhere in there is a human being who is suffering, a person who made bad choices. While I'm not trying to justify their behavior in any way, even for perpetrators of childhood sexual abuse, there is a human being in there that got so misguided that they were trying to get their happiness through these horrendous actions. After all, they are coming to work with us because they want to get better. This is an important distinction—we are not saying we are okay with their behaviors. We are not saying it's okay to keep doing those behaviors, but somewhere in there, can we get in touch with and influence that human being who wants a more workable and healthy way to lead a more fulfilling life?

ACCEPTANCE AND FORGIVENESS

Sometimes clients have trouble accepting themselves because of the things they have done in the past. Or they think they are supposed to forgive everyone who has ever hurt them. Acceptance also includes accepting the hurt, the anger, and the thoughts. It is not necessarily about feeling better about the past.

Sometimes it can be useful to talk to clients about the difference between acceptance (and self-acceptance) and forgiveness (and self-forgiveness). I once went to a great workshop on this topic given by a psychologist named Janis Abrahms Spring (2004). Even in the workshop, people argued with her about the difference between acceptance and forgiveness, but I felt the distinction that she made was very useful.

Forgiveness can really only happen if the person who harmed you attempts to repair the relationship, or tries to make up for the damage they created. In order for forgiveness to happen, the other person has to feel remorseful about their behavior, and make a conscious effort to make up for it.

However, sometimes the person is not sorry for what they did, or they don't care enough to make an effort to repair things, or they may be deceased. In that case, all you can do is accept the reality of what happened. Getting angry, wishing things were different, or fantasizing about something bad happening to the other person will not help anything, and only adds to our own misery.

Likewise, we have all done things in the past that we wish we hadn't done. If it's possible, we can do something to repair the damage and forgive ourselves. Otherwise, we can practice accepting that we did those things, and set our resolve toward what we can do from this point forward.

Ultimately, clients (and therapists too) come to realize that they have no choice but to accept things as they are in this moment. The past cannot be changed, and the future has not yet arrived. While this may sound depressing at first, it actually frees up an enormous amount of energy. Instead of fighting with reality, they can more fully focus on taking action toward their values.

To do this, it will be helpful to practice consciously and mindfully making contact with the present moment, which is the subject of chapter 7.

Just This Moment: Breaking Free from Future Worries and Past Regrets

People with anxiety spend so much time living in their heads that they end up missing out on their actual lives. Their minds are full of past regrets and future planning, and they wonder why their lives pass by so quickly. Mindfulness practices help us to get more in touch with the actual moments of our days, which helps us consciously and systematically build a meaningful life.

Though challenging at first, when anxiety can be investigated with interest and curiosity, we discover that there is nothing inherently terrible in the body sensations underlying the seemingly intense thoughts and emotions. We can learn to let go of the unnecessary battles and struggles with ourselves, and just take each moment as it comes.

This chapter will explore the problems of getting lost in past memories and caught up in imaginary futures. Through mindfulness exercises and worksheets, clients can learn concrete skills and a practical understanding of how to enrich their lives by living more fully in the present moment.

DOMINANCE OF THE CONCEPTUALIZED PAST AND FUTURE

When we are not mindfully in contact with the present moment, we get caught up in conceptualizations about the past and the future. If you're always in the past and the future in your head, then you're not going to be very flexible, because you're not going to be in touch with what is happening right now.

Anxiety occurs when the mind is comparing this time and place to somewhere or somewhen else. Somebody once sent me a funny cartoon. It had three different boxes. In the first box, it showed a man at work, but in the little thought bubble, it showed he was thinking about playing golf. In the next box it showed him playing golf, but in the thought bubble, he was thinking about having sex with his partner. In the last box, it showed him having sex with his partner, but he was really thinking about work. **People with anxiety have a tendency to be somewhere else in their minds, no matter what they are experiencing in reality.**

Growing up, a lot of us are taught to have a future focus. Alan Watts (2004), one of my favorite philosophers, talks about a trick that is played on us in this culture. We are told that all the good stuff is coming in the future. When we are small children, we can't wait until we're old enough to be able to go to school. After kindergarten, we'll be able to get into the first grade. We have to do well in the first grade, because we want to get into the second grade. We better do well in the second grade so we can get into the third grade, eventually getting into middle school and high school. High school is when it really counts, because we need a good grade point average so that we can get into college.

And of course, you better do really well in college, because you want to get into graduate school so you can live the glamorous lifestyle of a mental health professional! You better do well in graduate school so you sit through the licensure exam. You better study for that exam so that you can get licensed. Once you get licensed, then you will be able to get a job. Won't that be great? Once you have a job, then you will have money. Once you have money, then you will be able to buy all this cool stuff to make you happy, for a little while, and then you've got to buy more stuff. Then you've got to get a house, and then you have to fix up that house. Then you have kids, and you want them to do this too, so you work harder to make more money. And you take that promotion, because retirement is coming, and you need to put money away for the future.

Now, assuming you even live long enough to retire with your health intact, what do people want to do when they retire? Just be in the moment, and hang out with their friends, just like when we were kids. So, what was the point of that whole journey?

If you're a young person, here's a spoiler alert. Somewhere around middle age, you wake up one day and realize, "Hey, wait a minute, I've been tricked! **This _is_ my life! It's not _coming_. It's not _someday_. It's not in the future. I've been in it all along!**" You end up missing out on experiencing a lot of the moments of your life, because you are always thinking about the next thing. Even when something great happens, not to mention all the little things in daily life, you don't appreciate it, because you are always on to the next thing. And when you get to the next thing, you're on to the next thing, so you're never fully living in the present moment. Or, you postpone your enjoyment of the moment, because you keep telling yourself that you'll be happy after this happens, or after that happens, and you lose the capacity to be present.

We can also get lost in the past. Hindsight is 20/20, and we can remember all the mistakes we made, and be full of regrets about our choices. If we are not happy with our lives, instead of creating more of the life we want, we spend our time blaming others, or thinking, "If only things had been different."

People can get stuck believing the "good old days" were in the past, wishing they were still young. Of course, it might be natural to do that at times, but if we end up dwelling on those thoughts, we rob ourselves of the time we have right now. Then 10 years from now, we think, "I had it so great 10 years ago, but I wasted the time I had." We can also be very selective about what we remember. I can bring to mind really good times when I was younger, but when I really think about it, I can recall that those younger years also came with sadness, loneliness, and financial struggles.

Unless we make contact with the present moment, our lives will continue to slip away.

LIMITED SELF-KNOWLEDGE

When we are not mindfully in contact with the present moment, we are also not aware of ourselves. The thoughts and images in our minds are only representations, and we can only know reality through our senses.

Many people have a tendency to operate in a sleepwalking state, or in an automatic pilot mode, where they are barely aware of what they are thinking, feeling, or doing. People often engage in automatic pilot modes of thinking, emotionally reacting, and behaving. In certain contexts, these automatic tendencies are helpful, but other times they get people into trouble, and contribute to making situations worse.

I'm sure you've had clients who have been hurt badly in past relationships, so they learned to put up walls to keep themselves safe. While that might have been good when they were being taken advantage of, now they are doing it automatically, and complain that they are lonely. When you suggest they get out and meet new people, they get angry and tell you that people are stupid. They do not realize that their thoughts, reactions, and behaviors are contributing to their loneliness.

Without self-awareness, people also do not realize how they come across to other people. We all have met people who do not realize the effect they have on others, and they wonder why people avoid them. This is especially true for individuals with personality disorders, who lack a well-developed observing ego (Lester, 2018).

If you're not aware of your own internal processes, and you're not aware of the impact of your actions, you're not going to be very effective, and you're going to be inflexible.

MINDFULNESS: CONTACT WITH THE PRESENT MOMENT

Mindfulness, or contacting the present moment, counters our tendency to be lost in other times in our heads, and helps us be more aware of ourselves.

Mindfulness just means paying attention. Clients can practice exercises to strengthen this attentional capacity, which will be shared in the next few sections. This strengthened attention helps them become more self-aware. They can practice noticing their own thoughts, feelings, and body sensations to foster more internal self-awareness, and to notice how they react to their internal experiences. In the research, both clinicians and clients who practice mindfulness rate higher on scales of self-compassion (Birnie, Speca, & Carlson, 2010; Hollis-Walker & Colosimo, 2011; Kuyken et al., 2010; Neff, 2003). By noticing their own thoughts, emotions, and body sensations as they are, they begin to let go of battling with their own internal experiences.

Clients can also practice noticing the external environment, and how they come across to other people. This helps them develop the ability to flexibly adapt their behavior to the relationship or situation they are in to move toward their values. Paying attention helps you know when to persist and when to change your behavior, based on what the situation affords.

You can only pay attention in the present moment. The only time you can be flexible, and the only time you can do or experience anything, is in the present moment. Everything else is just an idea. **Because clients with anxiety are particularly prone to getting lost in their heads, we emphasize coming back in contact with this present moment, just as things are.** They may not like things as they are right now, but they're going to deal with things better if they are in touch with reality and are self-aware.

One of the ways that I illustrate this tendency to be lost in our heads is to talk about using a planner. I use the planner app on my phone, which is very convenient for setting meetings and appointment reminders.

A planner is a great tool, but has this ever happened to you? You wake up in the morning and look at your planner. (First of all, don't look at it first thing in the morning, let yourself wake a little bit.) You notice, "Oh my gosh! I've got 9 clients today, and I've got 27 reports that are overdue, and I've got 34 phone calls to return, and I've got 873 unopened emails!!!" You haven't even gotten out of bed yet, and you're already thinking, "Oh, this is going to be a long day! What was I thinking becoming a mental health professional! Maybe I should just quit and become a tree farmer!" Your stress fires up, and you carry it around all day long.

You can practice reminding yourself (and this does take practice): "Right now, in this moment, I'm just looking at my planner." All the rest of that stuff is only happening in your head. There better not be nine clients in your bed with you first thing in the morning!

In the next moment, you will put your planner down. Now, you're walking down the hallway, now you're drinking your coffee, and now you're driving your car. You get to the office, and now you're with this client, now you're with that client, and now you're with the next client. There is no need to carry around the whole day in your head in each moment.

As an interesting side effect, when you're more in the moment, you can actually be a lot more productive and efficient in your work, and yet, feel less busy. **Consider this: The feeling of busyness only comes when you are thinking about what you are *not* doing.** In a certain sense, it doesn't matter if you have a million things to do later or nothing to do. In this moment, you are just reading this book.

But if, in the back of your mind, you get lost in thinking, "I shouldn't be reading this. I've got 27 reports to write, 34 phone calls to make, and 873 emails to open," you will feel busy. If you want to write a report, just go write a report. But if while you're doing it, you're paying attention to "I hate writing these reports—I wish I were doing something else right now," you're going to feel stress, and you're not going to write the report very well. You just write some words, which form a sentence, which form a paragraph.

Now of course, it can be important to reflect on the past. You also need to set time aside to plan your day, and to triage what is most important to get done. But if all day long you get lost in thinking about what you are not doing, or about being somewhere where you are not, you will create excess stress and anxiety. **Anxiety often comes from thinking about what MIGHT happen in the future.**

Clients (like therapists) often feel overwhelmed by all the things they need to do. They can spend almost the entire session just listing all the problems they need to deal with. Sometimes I will literally interrupt the client and say, "Well, we can talk about those problems one at a time if you like. But let me remind you, right now, in this moment, you are just sitting in my chair, talking with me." It's amazing how quickly that can bring clients back into the moment, into what is happening right now. "When this session is over, you will be walking to your car. In a little while, you will be back at your office. Later tonight, you will be at home with your family. In your head, there is no limit to what you can deal with, but in reality, you can only be in this moment. You can just take all those problems one moment at a time."

People have a tendency to always be ready for the *next* moment, always rushing to the next thing. But ultimately, where are you going? People sometimes eat really quickly. Why? So they can take another bite, and then eat that really fast, so they can take another bite, and eat that really fast? The taste is right here. Where are you going? **You can only be where you are.** If you can't be in this moment, how are you going to be in the next moment, and in the next moment?

Of course, you can be in this moment, and still pay attention to the direction you want your life to go. I'm certainly not saying to just sit still in this moment. Sometimes I am asked, "Well, what about somebody who's *too* in the moment?" I tell them I have never met anyone who is too in the moment. Even the Dalai Lama and my Zen teachers are active in the world. Usually when I hear that, it is referring to a person's tendency to avoid responsibility. "I don't want to wash the dishes, I just want to be in this moment and play video games." That's avoidance.

Mindfulness is a very active, dynamic process. It's important to pay your bills. It's important to make goals. You can be in this moment and be very productive. It's about living in this moment as it unfolds into the next moment, moving in the direction of what matters in your life.

The following handout helps clients make contact with the present moment through the five senses.

Coming to Your Senses

With anxiety, you are often living in your head, caught up in endless worries about what might happen in the future, or you get lost in ruminations about how the past should have been different.

But in this moment, in this place where you are right now, things are often not as bad as your brain is thinking they might be.

Mindfulness is about noticing what is happening right now. But how do you do that when your brain keeps wanting to go elsewhere?

Here's the funny thing about all this present-moment stuff. A lot of people will say, "I need to be more in the moment. I need to get more in the moment." You know what the big joke is? You can't get out of the moment! Just try to get out of the moment!

The truth is, you're always in the moment. Why are you trying to get into it? You can't get out of it. Even when you are thinking about the past and the future, you are doing it right now, in this moment. **The problem is, we confuse all that mental representation with what we're experiencing here and now through our senses.**

In fact, people use the word "empirical" to talk about reality. Science is all about empiricism. Do you know what the word "empirical" literally means? Evident to the senses. I can see it. I can hear it. I can taste it. I can smell it. I can touch it. That's what empirical means. Guess what—**empirically speaking, nothing exists but this present moment!** It may sound a little philosophical when I put it this way, but you can come to experience this for yourself. You can't hear the future, and you can't smell the past—they only exist in your mind. Your senses can only experience reality in the present moment.

In our minds, the past goes back forever, and the future goes forward forever, and this present moment can seem like a tiny hairline instant that is always slipping away. However, when you pay attention, you realize that the opposite is true. The past only exists in your memory. You can't give me anything from the past—if you do, you are doing it right now in this moment. You can't touch the future. It's just an idea. **It's quite an amazing sensation to go from all these imagined other times to recognizing that you are just always in this vast present moment.**

Don't misunderstand what I'm saying—the future is a very useful idea. We need to make plans and set goals. It's also good to remember the past—to reminisce, and to learn from our mistakes. There may be times you consciously choose to sit in this moment and think about the past or the future. It's just helpful to remember that they simply don't exist to the senses. When that really sinks in, dropping the heaviness of all that mental baggage is a wonderful thing to experience.

The next time you feel overwhelmed with thoughts about the past or the future, practice coming to your senses. What do you see? What do you hear? What do you feel? What do you smell? What do you taste? You will notice that you can only experience your senses in the present moment, so allow each sense impression to anchor you into now. This is one of the reasons many people enjoy being in nature—it allows you to fully engage all your senses.

Be careful not to use this as a way to run away from distressing thoughts or feelings. Those may be part of this present moment too. You can just practice consciously coming into this moment through your senses when you find yourself lost in other times in your mind.

Read through this handout several times over the next few weeks. It may not make much sense to your thinking brain, but you might just wake up to something important about your life, and learn to relate differently to your anxiety.

Mindfulness versus Meditation

The word "meditation" often has a lot of baggage, and it can mean a lot of different things to different people. Technically, meditation is a very broad term that refers to a wide variety of methods for working with the mind. There are literally thousands of types of meditation. Mindfulness is a very specific type of meditation that focuses on paying attention in the present moment.

Sometimes it's useful to do formal mindfulness exercises, but not all clients will be interested in techniques that look like meditation. In fact, Russ Harris (2009) wrote an article called "Mindfulness without Meditation." For some clients, you might choose to not even use the word "mindfulness." The point is to foster the ability to pay attention in the present. You can help clients be more mindful in a conversational style. "What thoughts are showing up right now?" "How are you feeling in this moment?" "Are you noticing any sensations in your body?"

The following handout describes an informal practice that involves paying attention to the breath.

Just One Breath

When you struggle with anxiety, it can be easy to get caught up in your thoughts and worries, and literally forget to breathe. The stress response itself is physiologically tied to the breath. When you are stressed, you breathe more quickly and more shallowly from the chest, and this triggers your brain to release more stress chemicals to keep you ready to fight, flee, or freeze in order to deal with danger.

The good news is that even taking one deep breath from the belly literally shifts your body's stress response system and changes your brain chemistry. **And no matter how busy you are, you can always take a breath.**

I once went to a workshop that was focused on working with the breath. At the end, the instructor, Stephen K. Hayes, said, "Your homework assignment is to breathe six times a day." Of course, we all laughed. We breathe thousands of times a day—why would he say that?

While the number six was a bit arbitrary, his point was to observe what happens if you pause several times a day and take a deep breath. If you find yourself rushing from thing to thing all day long, just pausing to take one deep breath is a way of resetting yourself, and will even create a small physiological shift.

I once consulted with a neurology team that was studying people with epilepsy. They told me that if a new medication reduces seizures by even a small amount, they can sell it on the market as an anti-seizure medication. The team thought that surely stress reduction techniques could reduce seizures by that small amount. They wanted to teach people with epilepsy a technique called progressive muscle relaxation, which involves systematically tensing and relaxes muscles throughout the body.

They were able to recruit hundreds of volunteers, and gave them pagers. The first thing they needed to do was establish a baseline to find out how stressed out they were. They paged them at random times throughout the day, and asked them to write down how stressed they were feeling.

Guess what they found—the stress levels started going down before they could even do the "stress reduction" technique! **Just the act of pausing, noticing, and checking in with their stress actually helped to bring the stress down!**

Since we have a tendency to get really caught up in our busyness, **the challenge can be just remembering to remember to pause and take a breath.**

The good news is that you can find ways to associate certain things with remembering to take a breath. I once had a graduate student use an app on her phone to help her remember to pause. She set it to ring a digital bell at random times throughout the day. The "ding" reminded her to just pause for a few seconds and breathe deeply, then just go back to whatever she was doing. She found it so helpful, she said, "I find myself just hoping all throughout the day that the bell is about to go off." With a wink in my eye, I said, "Well you know, you can pause and come back into the moment anytime you want to. You don't have to wait for the bell to go off!"

The next time you hear a bird chirp, or a car horn, or the ding of a text message, see if you can remember to pause and take a breath. It may just create a small series of cascading shifts in your day to get you out of your head and into the present moment.

Structured Mindfulness Exercises

Some people do prefer to have structured mindfulness exercises that they can practice between sessions. There are a wide variety of mindfulness exercises, each with different emphases. You can find several free downloadable recordings on my website: www.psych-insights.com.

A simple but helpful mindfulness exercise that clients often find useful is called the three-minute breathing space, which comes from the Mindfulness-Based Cognitive Therapy protocol (Williams, Teasdale, Segal, & Kabat-Zinn, 2007). For one thing, when a client hears that the exercise is only three minutes long, it doesn't sound very intimidating, so they are more likely to start practicing it. Because it is shorter than other formal mindfulness practices, it is easier to incorporate throughout the day. Also, as you will see, even though it is short, it contains a lot of different pieces to exercise the client's ability to be mindful.

You can read the following script to the client, or they can read through the handout themselves at home. They can also download a free audio recording of this exercise from my website.

The Three-Minute Breathing Space

Checking in with ourselves is the first step to dealing with our lives and our emotions more consciously and proactively. As the name implies, the three-minute breathing space is a short exercise, which allows you to do it several times a day to develop more self-awareness. Once you notice things as they are, **you open up the chance to consciously respond instead of automatically react to what is happening.**

Because this is a short exercise, you can do it almost anywhere—lying on a couch at home, sitting at a desk at work, or you can slip off to the bathroom if you don't want anyone to see you. By the way, if there are people around, and you think it might look weird to sit still for three minutes, just hold your cell phone in front of you—no one would ever question that!

To begin, you might find it helpful to remind yourself, right now, **there is literally nowhere else that you could be.** You don't have to be doing something else more important for the next few minutes. Just **give yourself permission to drop into this moment as it is.**

The first minute of this exercise is to **check in with yourself.** We spend so much of our time thinking about or paying attention to other times, other places, and other people. Just check in with yourself to notice things as they are right now.

Start with your **physical body.** What sensations are you noticing right now? Do a quick scan from your head down to your toes. For just this moment, you don't necessarily have to analyze or fix anything—just notice. Become aware of the surface you are on, feel the clothing on your skin, and even notice if there is some tension or discomfort in your body. You can certainly move your body if you need to, but see if you can just notice what is already here as it is.

Then check in with your **emotional state.** Right now, in this moment, how are you feeling? Are you a little bit tired, or irritated, or happy, or some combination of things? How do you know how you are feeling? Are there places in your physical body that give you a clue about your emotional state? Again, for right now, you don't have to fix anything, analyze anything, or make it go away. Just give yourself permission to feel what you are already feeling.

At a more subtle level, see if you can **notice what you are thinking.** What thoughts or images are coming and going in your mind from moment to moment? Instead of getting lost in your thoughts, or carried away with them, can you just notice them as thoughts? You might even imagine you are watching your thoughts being projected on a movie screen. Instead of getting lost in the movie, with all the emotions and drama, can you step back and just notice the movie?

The second minute is to **feel your breath** as a way of gathering up the attention to sort of collect yourself, to center yourself, by focusing on one thing, in this case the breath. Rather than thinking about, or imagining the breath, can you get in touch with the actual physical sensations? Feel the stomach as it rises and falls. Or maybe you notice the air as it moves in and out of your nose. It's a little bit cooler when you inhale, and it's a little bit warmer when you exhale.

Chances are your mind is going to wander off, or get distracted by something. That's okay. That's just what minds do. See if you can notice when that happens, and without struggling with it, simply keep gently bringing your attention back to the breath.

For the third minute, expand your awareness out beyond the breath, to include the entire body, all at once. Instead of feeling like you are only a brain with something kind of dangling underneath, can you **feel yourself inside your entire body all at once**, with a broad awareness? Feel your *embodied* presence. And if you find it helpful, you can even remind yourself that whatever it is, or whatever is going on, it's already here anyway. **I can let things be exactly as they are for just this moment**.

Now, with a deep breath, let go of this exercise, and bring your attention back to the rest of the room.

At the end of this exercise, you might feel "better." Maybe the pause allowed your body, emotions, or thoughts to settle down, or you noticed that things are pretty good right now, and you have a sense of appreciation. Wonderful!

Maybe after doing this exercise, you feel "worse." Wonderful! No one wants to feel bad, but if that is your reality right now, it is best to notice it. If you became aware of lots of thoughts or anxious feelings, you might not have realized how anxious you were already feeling until you paused to check in. Maybe now you can choose to take a break. If you noticed muscle tension or pain, you can choose to go back to ignoring it, or you can do some stretching before it gets worse. Maybe you have to push through a work meeting first, but you can make a note to yourself to get more rest later. Noticing opens up a chance for you to go do some self-care, or at least to relate differently to your own experiences.

See if you can bring some of this awareness with you into the next few moments of your day. Ideally, you can practice this exercise several times a day to develop the habit of checking in with yourself more regularly.

Mindful Inquiry

As with all experiential exercises, it can be useful to process what the client experienced afterward. You can ask questions like "What did you notice during that exercise? Is what you just did any different from the way you normally relate to your experiences? What do you think this exercise has to do with relating differently to anxiety?" (Segal, Williams, & Teasdale, 2013).

During the inquiry process, it is important to model an attitude of curiosity and acceptance. Therapists have a tendency to want to fix, analyze, or make unpleasant experiences go away, but this can subtly reinforce avoidance. Staying present with a client's thoughts, feelings, and body sensations helps them learn to do it for themselves, facilitating their own sense of trust that they do not have to battle with their own experiences.

One thing clients often notice is how much their minds jump around when they sit still, sometimes referred to as "monkey mind." Because they often engage in avoidance strategies, their thoughts might seem to become more active when they pay attention. Normalizing this, and asking clients about the process of thinking rather than the content, models defusion.

Interestingly, sometimes clients develop a sense of appreciation after doing this exercise. They may notice they are not feeling anxious, or become aware of parts of their bodies that are not feeling pain. They come to realize how much their minds focus on what is wrong, and how they tend to ignore or take for granted the things that are going well.

Sometimes clients think the point of these mindfulness exercises is to feel better, or to become relaxed. While that can certainly happen, an attitude of doing mindfulness to feel better can end up reinforcing avoidance. Trying to "make yourself relax" creates a paradox of struggle. Sometimes clients feel better as a "side effect" of letting go of automatic struggles with their experiences, but the point is to notice things as they are, even if you don't like what you find.

Why would you want to do an exercise that might leave the client feeling worse? To increase awareness. If you do not notice your own internal experiences, it becomes easy to get lost in automatic struggles with them. **Noticing what is really going on allows you to make a conscious choice about what you want to do in this moment, if anything.**

For example, a client might say they feel worse after the exercise, because they didn't notice how much their head was hurting until they stopped to feel it. But chances are, it was already hurting. There may be a number of factors as to why it is hurting, but noticing it opens up options. They can stretch, take a pain reliever, or go back to ignoring it. Also, instead of being a nuisance, it becomes information. Maybe it suggests they had too much caffeine, they haven't been getting enough water or enough rest, or they need to do more stretching exercises.

Too often, clients ignore things until they seem overwhelming. If they notice tension in their neck and shoulders, they might be able to prevent a headache. Likewise, anxiety rarely tends to come out of nowhere. Clients can learn to catch it when it first begins, which is the subject of the next section.

Tip for Clinicians

Some people use mindfulness to feel better. It is wonderful if you feel better after a mindfulness practice, but the point is to get more in touch with feelings, not to get rid of them. If you always use mindfulness to help clients relax or get rid of unpleasant feelings, you might just be reinforcing avoidance, and making clients worse in the long run.

EXPLORING ANXIETY WITH CURIOSITY

Because anxiety is so unpleasant, clients tend to push it away, and create even more struggle. The next exercise involves a type of exposure therapy—moving into the anxiety itself with gentle curiosity. Curiosity is an attitude of exploration, and it is a different way of relating to experience than fighting and struggling.

It may be best to guide the client through this exercise in session a few times before they do it on their own. Ask the client to describe what they notice, and model a sense of curiosity about what they find. Remember that mindfulness is about paying attention. The point is not necessarily to make the anxiety go away, but to realize that the anxiety itself is not the enemy. Even though it is unpleasant, it is just what the body does, and adding struggle only exacerbates it. While this can be done while the client is currently experiencing anxiety, it can also be done when the anxiety is not very high as a way to practice turning toward internal experiences.

Getting to Know Your Anxiety

If you struggle with anxiety, you've probably been fighting it, pushing it away, or ignoring it for years. I'm also guessing that only helps temporarily at best.

In order to begin to make a shift in your life, it will be important to really get to know your anxiety. Not in the way that you may have struggled with it all this time, but in a new way. After all, how can anything change if you don't get to know exactly what you're dealing with?

Your anxiety has likely created a lot of problems in your life, so understandably you've been trying to get away from it. Yet, this tends to only increase the struggle in the long run. To create a shift, we will need to move into it. Get to know this so-called enemy, approaching it like a curious scientist.

Also, you want to start paying attention to how the anxiety manifests itself at different stages. It can be useful to think of anxiety like a water level. When the "water level" of anxiety is up to your nose, every little "wave" that comes along in life will feel like it is drowning you. But when the water level is down at your ankles, it will take a much bigger wave to knock you over.

Low-level Anxiety

Let's start with the earliest signs of anxiety, when the anxiety is metaphorically at your ankles. You might have trained yourself not to notice it, so see if you can pay attention to how you know it is there.

What tends to **trigger** low-level anxiety for you? Are there certain situations, thoughts, feelings, or body sensations connected to low-level anxiety?

_____

_____

_____

_____

What **thoughts** tend to show up when you are experiencing low-level anxiety?

_____

_____

_____

_____

What **feelings/emotions** tend to be present? Are there other subtler feelings besides anxiety?

_____

_____

_____

_____

What **body sensations** are present? Explore these like a scientist. Instead of just writing down "a bad feeling" can you get very specific? Notice such things as muscle sensations, tightness, burning, tingling, and heartbeat. Do they change with time?

_____

_____

_____

_____

Mid-level Anxiety

Next, let's explore what it is like when the anxiety is metaphorically up to your waist.

What tends to **trigger** mid-level anxiety for you? Are there certain situations, thoughts, feelings, or body sensations connected to mid-level anxiety?

_____

_____

_____

_____

What **thoughts** tend to show up when you are experiencing mid-level anxiety?

_____

_____

_____

_____

What **feelings/emotions** tend to be present? Are there other subtler feelings besides anxiety?

_____

_____

_____

_____

What **body sensations** are present? Explore these like a scientist, and be as specific and concrete as you can.

_____

_____

_____

_____

High-level Anxiety

Finally, let's look at the times when the anxiety is at its worst.

What tends to **trigger** high-level anxiety for you? Are there certain situations, thoughts, feelings, or body sensations connected to high-level anxiety?

_____

_____

_____

_____

What **thoughts** tend to show up when you are experiencing high-level anxiety?

_____

_____

_____

_____

What **feelings/emotions** tend to be present? Are there other subtler feelings besides anxiety?

_____

_____

_____

_____

What **body sensations** are present? Explore these like a scientist, and be as specific and concrete as you can.

_____

_____

_____

_____

Go through this worksheet a number of times. Reflect on the times you've felt these different levels of anxiety, and practice checking in with your "water level" throughout the day. You will likely notice more and more subtle things as you get increasingly familiar with these feelings.

Because anxiety can be so unpleasant, you probably trained yourself to not notice it throughout your day, only to end up drowning in it when it gets overwhelming. See if you can now practice paying attention to how you are doing with a sense of self-compassion. Even if you feel anxious about noticing the anxiety, just practice embracing that anxiety as well. After practicing this new way of approaching your anxiety, you may just realize that even if you don't like what you are experiencing, this anxiety is not your mortal enemy. After all, this is you, your own body doing what it is designed to do. It is okay to be you.

Chapter

8

Just Do It: Taking Committed Action

People with anxiety often get so stuck in battling their distressing thoughts and feelings that they stop doing the things that matter to them. They either give up on their futures, or they put off living until the conditions are "right." They tell themselves that as soon as all their problems are fixed, as soon as everything settles down, or as soon as their anxiety goes away, then they will live their lives. Unfortunately, for most people, they run out of lifetime before that ever happens, and they are full of regret when they look back over a wasted life spent waiting for the "right" moment to take action.

Insights and plans are useless without taking committed action. Long-term life goals can seem very big and very far away, but they manifest through the actions we take on a daily basis. This chapter will provide inspiration and practical worksheets for breaking down big-picture values into short-term, workable action steps.

UNWORKABLE ACTION

Unworkable action is another process that leads to inflexibility. If you keep doing the things that you have always done and expect a different result, you will become stuck. If the things that you are doing are not giving you the results that you want, it means what you are doing is unworkable.

Before they can become flexible, clients must let go of what is not working and do something different. When clients are stuck in unworkable action, go back to the creative hopelessness process, as described in chapter 3.

JUST DO IT: COMMITTED ACTION

Committed action stems from the behavioral foundation of ACT. Clients (and many therapists, by the way) spend a great deal of time thinking and talking, but nothing will change in the external world without some kind of physical action or movement.

As mentioned in the introduction, valued action predicts future drops in suffering, but drops in suffering do not predict future valued activity (Gloster et al., 2017). In other words, if you are experiencing a lot of problems, but take action anyway toward what matters to you, your distress is likely to go down. But if you tell yourself you're going to get rid of all your suffering first, and then do something important, you may never get around to doing it. Of course, it would be great if your anxiety went down when you commited yourself to taking action, but either way, the end result is that you are doing more of what matters to you. You can ask clients, **"Would you rather suffer with anxiety and have a meaningless life, or have a meaningful life that just happens to also have anxiety in it?"**

Once clients are in touch with their values, we can ask, "Are you willing to do something, to take some committed action, toward what you said is important to you?" The step can be very tiny, or it could be a big leap. The step is what is important, not the size of it. This is why it is called "committed action," because you can either take a step or not take it.

Clients often put off taking action, thinking, "Well, after I'm rich, or after I finish school, or as soon as all my anxiety goes down, then I will live my life." However, given that circumstances will never be ideal, the important question to ask clients is "What's one tiny thing you can do today to move you toward what is important in your life?" You can then expand it to tomorrow, next week, next month, and next year. The essential thing is to create momentum by getting started with little steps. This then creates a shift, leading toward bigger and bigger changes in patterns of behavior.

For example, you can ask a client, "Okay, you said your family was important. What is one thing you can do today, right after you leave my office, when you get home, that will bring you closer to your family?"

"Well, I guess I could play with my kids for five minutes."

"Wonderful! That's a very good goal to set. It's specific and attainable, and it will create movement toward having a better relationship."

Of course, the client's thinking will likely attempt to get in the way immediately. "Well, I'm willing, but I might feel anxious when I do it."

"You may not be able to control whether or not you'll feel anxious, but are you willing to play with them for five minutes anyway?"

More thinking is likely to pop up. "They're just going to say, 'You're only doing this because your therapist told you to.'"

Rather than arguing, shift to defusion, and get back to committed action. "Okay, so your brain is trying to tell you it might not go well, but are you willing to play with your kids for five minutes anyway, even if the thoughts pop up?"

These types of homework assignments can be called **life experiments**, which are opportunities to try out new behaviors to see if they produce different results. "As you know, if you keep doing what you have always done, you'll get what you've always gotten. Are you willing to experiment? You can't control the outcome, but you can control what you decide to do. Are you willing to do something different with your kids?"

Clients with anxiety get so stuck in battling their thoughts and feelings that they tend to stop doing meaningful activities, so therapists can emphasize behavioral activation. How you express this can vary depending on the client, but you might say, "Of course you don't want to have this anxiety! Nobody *wants* to be anxious. Yet, here it is, whether you want it to be or not. You've told me that everything you've done to try not to feel the anxiety, and to get rid of the thoughts, hasn't worked so far. Maybe you've been moving in the wrong direction, or attacking the wrong things. Instead of fighting these thoughts and feelings, let's get moving toward what matters to you."

One of the challenges is that when clients are feeling anxious, it is hard for them to remember what matters. Anxiety puts them in a survival mode, and distracts them from the bigger picture of living a meaningful life. You might therefore ask a client something like "What used to be meaningful to you?" or "Before the anxiety came, can you remember what you used to do for fun, or what you liked to do?"

I once had a client reply, "Well, I used to ride my bicycle, and sometimes I really miss it, but I don't feel like riding it anymore."

"Wonderful. Here's what I want you to do. When you go home today, I want you to get out your bicycle and ride it just once around the block."

"I might feel anxious," came his automatic thought.

"You feel anxiety every day anyway. Would you be willing to feel it and just ride your bike for a few minutes today?"

"It won't help," he quickly replied.

"Notice your mind trying to protect you by thinking it won't help. Would you be willing to just ride your bike once around the block when you get home anyway?"

Clients often let the anxiety make their choices for them. They also get endlessly caught up in fighting their thoughts, answering them, justifying them, and arguing with them. They can learn to just have the anxiety, and to just let the thoughts say or do whatever they want, and to simply go toward what matters. It is an amazing visceral experience to realize that even with anxiety and anxious thoughts, you can still move your feet toward what matters to you. That is pretty much all of ACT in a nutshell—notice the thoughts, notice the emotions, and do what matters to you in this moment.

The next two worksheets are designed to help clients develop specific behavioral steps to take toward their values. While we can help clients plan out some action steps, they will ultimately be much more committed to moving toward the goals that they pick for themselves.

Just One Thing

When we think about our big-picture values, they can often seem distant and disconnected from our daily lives. We have thoughts like "Someday I'll have a more fulfilling career," "I sure wish I was a better parent," or "I hope I can eventually be more spiritual."

Well, we can only live in this moment today. While it is very important to plan out steps for larger goals (as you can do in the next worksheet), we can live our values in small but very important ways on a daily basis.

For example, I want to someday build my own airplane, but I'm not in a place to do that right now. So, each night before I go to bed, I read a couple of pages from a magazine about kitplanes.

I value spirituality, but it doesn't have to become a huge, unattainable thing. Today, I can read something inspiring, meditate, watch the trees outside my window, or express compassion or kindness to someone near me.

I travel a lot and can't always be a good father for my daughter, but each day I make sure I tell her that I love her and ask about her day. When I'm home, I make a little time to take a walk or do some activity with her.

Think about the big things in your life that are most important to you. What is one thing you can do today, and maybe each day this week, that will be in alignment with what is important to you?

_____

_____

What thoughts might come up when you are about to do that?

_____

_____

What feelings might arise when you are about to do that?

_____

_____

It would be great if you felt good before you did that action, but would you be willing to do it even if you had uncomfortable feelings or negative thoughts?

_____

_____

Consider this as a behavioral experiment. Just do the action each day for a week, and notice what happens. You can't control the outcome, but you can choose to do something important to you, even if it is something very minor. If you wish, you can add several small things to this list, not as things that you *have* to do, but perhaps as things you can look forward to doing.

Setting SMART Goals

In the worksheet on values, you clarified the big-picture things that are important in your life. Now that you have some direction for your life, it is important to set goals that provide specific and concrete steps to move you that way. SMART goals are:

S = Specific (instead of vague)

M = Measurable (how you know when you've achieved it)

A = Achievable (break big goals down into smaller ones that are attainable)

R = Relevant (the goal should be connected to the value that is important to you)

T = Timely (set a date to make it happen)

Each goal should be a small step to take you toward your value. If it's too big, you may never get around to it. For example, if family is one of your values, spending lots of time with family after you retire may be pretty far off, and is also a bit vague. You can start with taking a walk with your family around the park today, going to a movie this weekend, and planning out the next vacation.

Also, as you go through this worksheet, watch out for what are called "unconscious person goals." If an unconscious person can do it better than you can, it's not a good goal to have. If you say, "I don't want to feel anxiety," well, an unconscious person is really good at not feeling anxiety. Maybe what you are saying is that you don't want anxiety to interfere with what's important to you in your life. What is important enough to you that you would do it even if you felt some anxiety?

Take some time to go through the worksheet below. Make sure you are listing SMART goals. For example, if health is a value, one of your goals might be exercise. To be **specific**, list exactly what you want to do, like walk on a treadmill. To make it **measurable**, you can set the goal to be walking three times a week. To make it **achievable**, you might limit the walking to 20 minutes each day. Because walking is healthy, this goal is **relevant**. You can make it **timely** by planning to walk on Mondays, Wednesdays, and Fridays, starting this week. If it is a one-time goal, like walking in a 5K event, you can set the date you want to achieve it by, like the end of next month.

Value

First, identify the big-picture value that you want to set some goals toward:

_____

_____

Short-term Goals

What goals can you set to move you in the direction of this value in the next few weeks, and the next few months? Be as specific as you can. Make sure they are relevant and achievable.

_____

_____

_____

_____

How will you know when you have achieved each goal? (Measurable)

_____

_____

By what date do you want to achieve each goal? (Timely)

_____

_____

Medium-range Goals

What goals can you set to move you in the direction of this value in the next year or two? Be as specific as you can. Make sure they are relevant and achievable.

_____

_____

_____

_____

How will you know when you have achieved each goal? (Measurable)

_____

_____

By what date do you want to achieve each goal? (Timely)

_____

_____

Long-term Goals

What goals can you set to move you in the direction of this value a few years from now, or even a decade or two from now? Be as specific as you can. Make sure they are relevant and achievable.

_____

_____

_____

_____

How will you know when you have achieved each goal? (Measurable)

_____

_____

By what date do you want to achieve each goal? (Timely)

_____

_____

Repeat the above process for any other life values you have.

Go through this worksheet several times for each value, and make adjustments to your goals as you begin to assess how workable or achievable they are. Also, check in with your goals every so often to make sure they are still relevant to your life values. Goals can change or be adjusted over time, especially when you are clear about the direction you want for your life.

As you make your goals, be sure you are getting in touch with what matters to you, and are not just doing things to impress others. Don't make your goals so big that you fail and feel bad. Create goals that inspire you to move forward toward something that matters. You are creating a roadmap to a fulfilling life.

INCREASING WILLINGNESS

Clients may come up with wonderful plans and action steps, but those things are useless if clients are not willing to do them. It is important to pay attention when clients are only "trying," or are waffling about whether or not to take an action step. You can only take a step or not take a step—there is nothing in between.

I worked with a young college student named Thomas, who had a lot of anxiety. When he first came to me, he said, "I can't attend any of my classes. I'll start the semester off okay, but then I get anxiety, and I think, 'I'll just go tomorrow, or I'll go next week.' The next thing I know, half the semester is over, and it's too late to recover, so I have to drop the class. Then I'm embarrassed that I've lost all this money for dropping the class. I know that whenever I just go to class, everything is fine, but most of the time, as I'm about to walk into class, I feel anxious, so I just keep walking."

This pattern of avoidance is a very common trap with anxiety. I decided to simply ask him, "When you think about going to class tomorrow, does that feeling come up right now?"

Thomas shifted in his seat. "As soon as you even ask me that, I get all anxious about going there."

Instead of me talking him out of the anxiety, I said, "As long as it's here, would you be willing to explore it?"

With a deep breath, Thomas said, "Okay, let's do it."

"Let's invite the anxiety into the room right now, and just investigate it a little. Where do you feel it in your body? What thoughts are here with it?" With some clients, just moving into anxiety often creates a shift in how they relate to it, but Thomas seemed to be stuck in an old pattern.

I decided to use the file cabinet technique. "Let me ask you—is this a new feeling, or an old feeling? In other words, does this feeling only seem connected to going to your college classes, or does this seem like an old familiar feeling you might have felt years ago?"

"It's definitely an old feeling," Thomas quickly replied.

"If you're willing, let's just do an experiment right now. I want you to see if you can remember a time in your past when you felt this exact same anxiety that you are feeling right here in this room. Now, it can be almost any time, but it's best if you can come up with one of the youngest times in your life that you felt this way."

Memories related to his mood state began easily coming to mind. He began describing a memory of being in grade school. In front of the whole class, he spilled a drink on his pants. All the kids pointed at him, laughing, and started calling him "pee-pee pants." After that day, he felt anxiety every time he went to class.

Since it is easier to give a younger self compassion, I had him imagine he could go back in time to comfort that younger self. The grade-school-aged self also expressed how impressed he was with everything the older self had already done with his life.

At the end of the exercise, Thomas exclaimed, "Holy cow! After all these years, every time I go into a college classroom, I feel like that kid in grade school that spilled a drink on himself!" He became fired up when he had made this discovery, and said, "I think I'll go to class tomorrow!"

"Well, what do you mean, you *think* you're going to go to class tomorrow? Are you going to go to class tomorrow or not?"

Thomas responded, "I'm 80 percent sure I'm going to go to class tomorrow."

Since we had good rapport, I literally start laughing. "What do you mean 80 percent? Do you mean you're going to leave an arm behind and only 80 percent of you is going to go there? You're either going to go, or you're not going to go. I don't care if you go to class or not—it's your life. But are you going to go, or not go?" Thomas just cracked up laughing.

Sure enough, Thomas went to class the next day. Once he started going, his grades picked up, and his behavior became self-reinforcing. He later told me, "I don't know why I was so afraid to go in the first place!"

It is important to get clients to commit to some small action—to commit to themselves, not to the therapist or anyone else. If they are not 100 percent committed, you can explore what is getting in the way. You can simply ask, "You say you're 80 percent certain now. What would it take to make that 100 percent?"

Now if they are really waffling, there are two possibilities to consider. One is that **they have not found a big enough value, a big enough reason** to be willing to be uncomfortable and take action.

The second possibility is that **the step is too big for them** in this current moment. It is much better to build small, progressive successful steps than to have such a big step that it is continuously postponed. In the above example, had going to class been too much, I might have said, "Would you be willing to just put one foot on campus? Just drive up, put one foot on the campus, and then go back home?" If not, then maybe just getting in the car. After he achieved those, he could set a goal to put two feet on campus, take ten steps, etc. We are building larger and larger patterns of behavior to move toward the client's values.

Sometimes clients will bargain with you. This is what they have likely been programmed to do to avoid their anxiety, so turn that into a conversation. This helps to model defusion and acceptance. "You said you were willing to stand on campus for five minutes, but now you are saying three—notice what your brain is doing. It sounds like it is waffling a little bit. Are you feeling anxiety right now? I'm fine with three minutes, if that's what you decide to do, but just notice what your mind is doing, because next it might say two, then one minute. You said you would do it tomorrow, but next it might be a week from now, or next month. We can bargain with that a little bit, but **I want you to decide what you would be willing to do based on what is important to you, not based on your thoughts or your anxiety.**"

That movement is critical for clients to start shifting and changing. **The only way to be different is to start doing things differently.**

Clients may then say, "I'll try." The next handout discusses the problem of "trying" (Hayes, 2007; Hayes, Strosahl, & Wilson, 2012; Watts, 2004).

Just Do It!

When you are ready to finally take some action to move you toward creating a more fulfilling life, obstacles can arise to taking those first steps. Here are some things to consider.

The Problem with Trying

People often say, "I'll give it a try." But there is a problem with the word "try."

In fact, do an experiment with me right now. Try to pick up this book or device and try to hold it over your head right now.

Did you pick it up and hold it over your head? I didn't say pick it up, I said *try* to pick it up. What does try mean? Usually trying is just a feeling of straining yourself, and nothing happens. You either pick it up, or you don't pick it up. As the Jedi Master Yoda said, "Do, or do not, there is no try."

And versus But

It can also be tempting to let your anxiety decide whether or not you will take an action step. For example, if you really want to see your family at a party, you might think, "I want to go to the party, **but** I might feel anxious when I get there." You make the anxiety the reason not to go.

Watch what happens when you change the word "but" to "and." "I want to go to the party, **and** I might feel anxious when I get there." In other words, you don't need to make having anxiety the condition of whether or not you want to go. Ask yourself, "Since this is really important to me, am I willing to bring the anxiety with me to the party?"

Your anxious feelings are not alien invaders from somewhere else. Your own body is doing what it is designed to do. You don't have to like it, but are you willing to be anxious, **and** do what matters, because it's moving you in the direction of the life you want to live?

If you just go to the party, your anxiety is likely to go down, and that would be a nice bonus. Yet, whether it comes down or not, you just taught yourself that you can still live your life, even if the anxiety is there.

The Limitations of Thinking

It can also be tempting to let the thoughts in your head tell you when and how to do things. Sometimes thoughts are helpful at planning, but they do not have to control your actions.

Imagine I am in front of you, holding my hand in a fist. Can you tell me in words how to open my hand? When I ask people this, they say something like, "Just stretch out your fingers." Then I ask, "How do I stretch out my fingers?" They say, "Tell your brain to send a signal to your fingers." I reply, "How do I tell my brain to send a signal to my fingers?" At which point, they get very annoyed, but you get the point. You can't explain it in words, you just do it. You don't have to wait for thinking to tell you how—you just do it.

In fact, try this—say out loud, "I cannot open my hand," and then open your hand. Were you able to open your hand, even when your words or thoughts said you couldn't? Looks like your own thoughts cannot stop you from taking action—that's an important insight! **There is no need to talk yourself into taking action, you can just do it.**

Who's in Charge?

Of course, those strong emotions and loud thoughts can seem very intimidating, so it's understandable that for years you've stopped doing things that matter to you. But that only seems to work temporarily at best—I'll bet the anxiety and the distressing thoughts have not permanently gone away using that strategy.

Sometimes thoughts are trying to help you by giving you a strategy. Sometimes your anxiety is trying to help by warning you to be careful about how you do something. **Thoughts and feelings can be very important advisors, but they tend to make terrible dictators.** Ultimately, *you* decide what you want to do based on what matters to you— the thoughts and feelings don't have to be in charge.

If you find yourself not taking action, there are likely two reasons. One, you don't have a big enough reason, so think about what you want your life to be about. Two, you may be taking too big a step. Maybe take a smaller step, or just do something for a shorter period of time. **Research shows that telling yourself, "I'll just do it for five minutes" can help with procrastination.** The point is to just get moving toward the life you want to live.

As the late Zen master Seung Sahn was fond of saying (long before Nike®), **just do it!**

ACTING WITH ANXIETY: EXPOSURE

Behavioral activation is an important component of traditional exposure therapies. In classic forms of exposure, the client faces the situation that creates anxiety, it gets worse (the extinction burst), and the client waits for it to pass. The point is to reduce the unpleasant feeling.

ACT takes a slightly different point of view on the exposure process. Trying to get rid of anxiety sometimes creates more struggle with it. It certainly is wonderful when the anxiety goes down, but the goal of ACT is not to get rid of the anxiety, it is to become more flexible (Hayes, 2008). To be willing to feel anxious if it is in the service of something that is important. Certainly, nobody wants to feel uncomfortable, and we are not asking them to feel discomfort for its own sake, but in the service of moving toward their values.

Before exposure therapy, clients tend to have a narrow and inflexible way of reacting, which is to avoid or struggle with anxiety when it shows up. **After exposure therapy, clients have increased psychological flexibility.** They can still avoid if they choose, but they can also feel the anxiety and go to a party. They can feel anxiety and talk to people. They can have anxiety and also drive to work.

This is an important lesson for clients—that their anxiety doesn't have to disappear before they can take action. Even if you are terrified of spiders, if there's a poisonous one walking straight at your baby, my guess is that you would smash it with your hand if you had to (followed by an "Ooo—ick!" sound and running to wash your hands). That baby is more important than your fear of the spider.

The question for our clients is "What is important enough to you that you are willing to take action toward it even when you feel anxious?" If someone has a fear of dirt, it might not be a big deal if you live in the middle of a city. You would not be motivated to do exposure work. But if you live on a farm, and gardening is important to your family, you don't want to lock yourself away from your family. Even if you get anxious about the thought of touching dirt, would you be willing to do it if it means you will be closer to your family?

I use a swimming pool metaphor to explain exposure therapy, but we have to be careful when using it not to imply that the discomfort must completely go away. Most clients can relate to this metaphor in the sense that they can stay with some discomfort for a while, and fighting with it doesn't help.

Have you ever gone on vacation with your family, and they all want you to come into the hotel swimming pool? You stick your foot in the water, and it's cold. You'd rather sit in the lounge chair and watch everyone else, but your family wants you to come in and swim with them. You know that if you just go in the water, and stay in the water, you'll be fine.

When you first go in, you will feel worse than you did before, which is called the **extinction burst**. You will feel even colder when you first get in the water. But if you are willing to stay in the water and let it be cold, and you don't fight the cold, you can focus on enjoying the time with your family.

To stretch the analogy, traditional exposure therapy gives you two options: flooding and systematic desensitization.

Flooding is what my children like to do. They cannonball into the water, freeze all over their little bodies, but after a minute or two, they're having a fantastic time and don't feel cold at all.

Then you've got those of us who prefer **systematic desensitization**. You prolong your torture by going over to the steps. You put your left foot in and wait for it to adjust, then you put your right foot in and wait for it to adjust. And you get mad at the kids if they splash you while you are doing this.

You can do it either way. The point is that you go in. You may feel worse, but if you just stay in the water, you are able to enjoy swimming with your family.

The worst thing you can do at the swimming pool, or with your anxiety, is to jump in, and react with, "Ahh! This is uncomfortable! I don't like to be uncomfortable!" and jump back out immediately. Then you reproach yourself with "This is silly, I'll try again," followed by "Ahhh! It's uncomfortable!" If you jump in and out repeatedly, or you are always rushing to get to the other side of the pool to quickly jump back out again, you only fuel the sense of struggle, and are less likely to be focusing on what matters in your life.

I once had a client take this metaphor to another level. After I explained it to her, she said, "Gee, maybe I've been standing on the side of the swimming pool my whole life! While I'm standing on the side, I don't have to be as uncomfortable, but I've been missing out. I've just been watching everybody else have a good time!" That insight was a turning point for her.

Once a client finds that willingness to move into the discomfort for the purpose of something more important, the next step is to develop some concrete behavioral goals. If they hate dirt, but they really want to be outside with their kids, collaboratively translate that into specific goals. They might choose to stand outside for ten minutes, just watching their kids play. The next week, they can go outside for 15 minutes. They might choose to put their hands in dirt for two minutes. Small, concrete, specific goals are very important to get movement. And since each of those actions will be uncomfortable, remember to link them to their values.

Exposure techniques can be helpful for both external and internal experiential avoidance.

Exposure for External Avoidance

External experiential avoidance occurs when clients avoid people or situations that trigger feelings of anxiety. Of course, this is sometimes a good thing. There are certain people and certain situations that we definitely want to avoid. If I'm standing on the roof of a building, and I'm having a thought about jumping off, I'm going to feel anxious. That anxiety will prevent me from jumping off the roof.

Avoidance itself is not bad. But if I feel anxious about going to my daughter's school dance, and I decide to avoid going because I don't want to feel anxious, I may be damaging the relationship I have with my daughter. In this case, I will choose to feel anxious because my daughter is important to me.

Exposure for external avoidance can be live (in vivo) or imaginal.

I once did an **in vivo exposure** for a client named Jamie with OCD. When she first came in, she talked about her pattern of fighting her thoughts. When she had a distressing thought, she would try to calm herself down with a positive thought, but that would only produce more negative thoughts. We practiced defusion exercises, but Jamie's habit of fighting her thoughts was deeply ingrained.

She came into my office one day for an emergency session. She had been in her kitchen that morning, opened up a drawer, and saw a big knife. A thought flashed through her mind of stabbing her kids and stabbing herself, and of course she immediately became anxious.

Jamie was tearful as she described it to me. "Oh my gosh! Why would I think that?! I love my kids! I would never want to hurt them!" She could not stop thinking about not thinking about it.

To normalize her feelings, I said, "As funny as it sounds, feeling anxiety about this is what your brain is supposed to do. Your brain randomly created a picture of stabbing your kids, and then it stamped that picture with anxiety, screaming, 'Don't do that!' If you had a picture of stabbing the kids, then thought, 'Oh, that sounds like a pretty good idea!' then I'd be really nervous about you!" Jamie smiled through her tears.

Because we had good rapport, I felt like she was ready for some direct exposure. "Now please feel free to say 'No,' but I just happen to have a small pocketknife in my desk. Would you be okay with me taking it out and just putting it next to me on the chair here?"

She was sitting about four feet across from me, but still looked a little uneasy at first. "Okay, if you think it will help, I trust you."

I pulled out the knife, opened it up, and set it down on the chair next to me. I just let it sit there as we continued the session. A few minutes later, I said, "You know what I noticed? You didn't lunge at that knife, and then try to stab me with it. That's pretty interesting."

Jamie smiled. "Actually, it doesn't bother me at all right now."

She appeared ready for more. "Again, please feel free to say 'No,' but would you be willing for me to put this on the couch next to you?"

Jamie shifted in her chair and her eyes got big. "Oh, I don't know—that seems a lot harder!" After a few moments, with a deep breath, she said, "Okay—I'm willing. Let's do it!"

I gently placed the open knife next to her on the couch, and we continued the session. A few minutes later, I said, "I'm noticing that you didn't grab that knife and start stabbing yourself. Interestingly, you had a *thought* about stabbing, but those thoughts, and the anxiety they create, can't *make* you do anything. Those thoughts are only in your head, and your anxiety is just a natural thing that your body does."

Of course, I wouldn't do an exposure like that with certain clients, like those with antisocial personality disorder or thought disorders. It was obvious to me that she was only having thoughts, not intentions (and since I'm a ninja, I could always disarm her if I needed to).

For some clients, **imaginal exposure** may be easier or more practical. I once worked with a woman with OCD named Clarice who became very afraid of driving her car, because she was always worried that she was going to run over somebody. Everyone who drives will hit a bump once in a while, especially with all the potholes in downtown streets. For Clarice, when she hit a bump, a thought would pop up in her head, "What if that was a person I just ran over?" That thought would make anyone anxious. Clarice knew the thought was ridiculous, but it caused a little anxiety, nonetheless.

Most of us would feel a little anxiety if we had that thought and just keep driving. But since Clarice really didn't like the anxiety, she knew that if she turned the car around to check, she would know for sure. When she turned around to check, there would be nobody there, and the anxiety would go down, negatively reinforcing the checking behavior. Because her action dropped the anxiety, it made her more likely to want to do it again.

After checking, Clarice would continue driving along, and another thought would pop up, like, "Maybe I was looking left, and the body was actually on the right side!" Then, she would argue with herself, "Oh stop it! That's ridiculous! I wish I hadn't had that thought!" Even knowing the thoughts were ridiculous, they sparked anxiety, and since she didn't like anxiety, she would just go back and check, and the anxiety would temporarily go down. It took her so much time to get anywhere that she tried to avoid driving as much as possible.

Since I wasn't going to drive around with her looking for people to run over, we did imaginal exposure. While some clients have trouble with imagery, some clients respond very well with this method. I hooked Clarice up to a heart rate monitor to get a sense of how she was doing, and I had her imagine she was walking to her car, getting into her car, and driving around. Her heart rate went up a little at times, but just the thought of driving did not make her very anxious.

I quickly realized that driving didn't bother her, it was the thought of running over someone. Since we had good rapport, I suggested, "You seem to be doing fine, so if you're up for it, let's work on the scarier stuff." Clarice nodded in agreement. "I want you to imagine you're driving along, and suddenly, a man steps out in front of your car."

At this point, her heart rate definitely went up. "You slam on the brakes, but you just know that there is no way you will stop in time." Her heartbeat was elevated, but still fairly low, so I continued. "Your car is skidding… the man looks up with a scared look on his face… the bumper hits his knee… he bounces on your hood… his face is pressing against the windshield…"

At one point, Clarice said, "Oh my gosh, my heart feels like it's going to explode. It's just racing so fast. Are you sure this is okay?"

"Of course, we can stop anytime you like, but why don't you open your eyes and look at your heart rate?" Her heart rate was 85. I said, "You know, a lot of people have resting heart rates above 85, so your heart is doing fine."

Clarice was pleasantly surprised. "Wow, I thought my heart was really racing. I can't believe it's just 85."

While her anxiety did come back down, there was a deeper point to this process. Clarice's OCD behavior was due to a fear of running over somebody. By exposing her to that thought, she learned she didn't have to try not to think about it anymore, so she stopped giving that thought power. She learned she could just bring those thoughts, and the anxiety, along for the drive.

Exposure for Internal Avoidance

Internal experiential avoidance involves trying to run away from unpleasant thoughts, emotions, memories, and sensations going on within oneself. When doing so disrupts the quality of clients' lives, they can move into those experiences to learn how to relate to them differently.

As mentioned in chapter 1, ruminations and worries can actually be contributing factors to this internal avoidance cycle. Because people don't want to feel the anxiety, they go off in their heads with thinking, which distracts them from the feeling. The thoughts spark more anxiety, so they want to avoid that by thinking more. In a sense, it's like getting addicted to thinking. Taking a drink of alcohol lowers anxiety, negatively reinforcing the desire to take another drink. Going off into their heads doesn't take away the anxiety, but it temporarily lowers it, because they don't feel it as sharply when they are in their heads. This is why people want to keep doing it, and they can literally get stuck in this avoidance cycle their entire lives.

We all know that if people are afraid of specific things or situations, exposure can be helpful. But for clients with generalized anxiety disorder (GAD), how do you expose them to everything? It may be helpful to conceptualize that an important component of GAD is anxiety about feeling anxiety. The anxiety is what drives the client's choices. If they think about going to a party, that makes them feel anxious, so they don't go to the party, because they don't like anxiety. Driving a car, that makes them anxious, so they don't want to drive a car. Dealing with finances, that brings up anxiety, and they don't want that anxiety, so they let somebody else deal with that. Their lives become very restricted, and they become very inflexible, because they want to avoid feeling the anxiety or having anxious thoughts.

Mindfulness, defusion, and acceptance exercises can be very helpful for internal avoidance. **Sometimes committed action involves bravely diving into the source of the anxiety.** Clients can learn to investigate their thoughts, anxiety, and body sensations with curiosity. Anxiety is a response of the sympathetic nervous system and therefore begins in the physical body. When clients learn to stay with the sensations in their bodies, and let go of the need to fight or control their own experiences, they don't need to avoid the anxiety by thinking. They don't need the compulsive thinking to distract them from the anxiety going on in the body if they are no longer afraid of their own sensations.

This is true even for health anxiety. Health anxiety can be particular challenging for therapists, as logically arguing with clients often can make them caught up even more in spirals of "Yeah, but…" and "What if?" Recent research on health anxiety suggests that process types of approaches, like ACT, can be more effective than disputing the content of the thoughts (Mojtabaie & Gholamhosseini, 2014; Tauber et al., 2019).

I had a client named Jerome come in to see me a few months after he suffered a serious heart attack known as a "widow maker," which has a low survival rate. Luckily, he just happened to be in the right place at the right time to get immediate treatment, so he survived. He naturally had a lot of anxiety about his health. After talking with him a little while, it became apparent that he tended to do a lot of thinking and ruminating about his health, so I decided to dive into the anxiety itself.

I asked Jerome if he would be willing to try something different, and he readily agreed. I asked, "Right now, in this moment, how anxious are you feeling on a scale of 1 to 10?" He said, "7."

Now, if you use those subjective units of distress scales (SUDS), I highly recommend you ask this follow-up question. I said, "How do you know it's a 7? Is there a sensation in your body telling you how anxious you are?" Even asking that question is a sort of exposure technique, mindfully moving into the experience.

After a few moments, Jerome said, "Well, I'm feeling the scar from my surgery, and my heart is beating really quickly."

I modeled staying present. "Okay, so you noticed the scar, and you noticed your heart beating. If you're willing, I'd like you to just keep your attention on those places for a little while. Instead of fighting with them or enduring them, I want you to investigate them like a curious scientist, trying to notice and learn as much as you can."

"As you do this," I continued, "you might notice your thoughts going back to the heart attack, or you might start thinking about what you're going to do when you go back to work. You don't have to stop or change the thoughts, just notice them, and gently bring your attention back to the sensations that are here in your body right now."

After a few more moments, I said, "Understandably, you've spent months either ruminating about or avoiding this feeling in your heart. You've given up important things in your life trying not to feel this. Let me ask you, now that you are sitting with them, gently holding them with your attention, is there anything about the sensations in the scar and in your heart beating that you just have to get rid of?"

"Well, I don't like them," Jerome quickly responded.

"Of course you don't like them, but is there really anything in them, exactly as they are now, that you just absolutely cannot have? In other words, as you feel the scar and your heart beating quickly, are these things your enemies?"

"Well, no, I guess not." Jerome sounded more measured in his words. "My heart is just doing what it does."

"Okay, so just notice your heart doing what it does for a few more moments."

After a few minutes, Jerome's anxiety dropped down to a 3, which really surprised him. Even though some anxiety was still there, he was able to let go of the struggles that were amplifying it. It's also important to note that even if the anxiety doesn't come down at all, clients can come to realize that they don't have to struggle to avoid their own body sensations.

The last thing most clients would think to do is move more directly into their experiences, because they often get worse at first. However, we can model staying present, and guide clients to explore and stay with their own experiences. **Very often what they find is not what they "thought" they would find.**

Tip for Clinicians

Exposure therapy can often be difficult for clinicians, because we are trained to help clients feel better. However, trying to "fix" or get rid of the client's anxiety during an exposure session will only reinforce avoidance. It is important to model staying present with the thoughts and feelings that show up, even if we ourselves get uncomfortable.

The following Tin Can Monster Exercise is a type of exposure exercise that can be useful for a wide variety of anxiety issues (Hayes, Strosahl, & Wilson, 2012). As with some of the other exercises in this workbook, it is best to guide the client through this a few times before asking them to do it on their own.

Tin Can Monster Exercise

When you struggle with anxiety, it can feel like you are facing an overwhelming monster. If you were to face a loud, scary, 30-foot-tall monster, you might think that all you could do is run and hide from it. Hiding from it might keep you safe, but a life spent hiding is not very fulfilling.

When you see that huge monster, you might think it's just too much to deal with. Likewise, your anxiety probably can seem so overwhelming that it may feel like there is nothing you can do but try to avoid it.

But when you look closely, even gigantic monsters are only composed of smaller parts. This metaphorical monster is only made up of tin cans, string, and bubble gum. **If you turn to face it, you don't have to take on the whole thing at once.** You can disassemble him one piece at a time.

Likewise, even though your anxiety seems huge, you can learn to face it and just investigate one piece at a time. This opens up the opportunity to relate in a new way to all the factors that contribute to the anxiety.

For this exercise, find a quiet place where you can be alone for about 15 minutes or so. Get in touch with your "observer self," that part of you that is aware of your own experiences. There is a bigger sense of who you are that is aware of what you are feeling, what you see, and what you hear. There is a part of you that can objectively observe your own thoughts, emotions, memories, and body sensations. Take a few moments to get in touch with that observing self, which has been there all your life.

Now, turn and face any anxiety that is already here. How intense does it seem to you on a scale of 1-10, with 1 being no anxiety, and 10 being the worst anxiety you can imagine?

_____

When you gave it that number, where did you feel it in your body? Like a curious scientist, take a few moments to explore your own **body sensations**. What physical sensations are you experiencing? Move your awareness through your body—what do you notice in your feet? Legs? Hips? Torso? Arms? Head? Be as descriptive as possible— notice tingling sensations, tightness in muscles, the speed of your breathing, etc. No need to fix them or change them, and you don't have to like them, just acknowledge them as they are, like saying "hello" to family members.

_____

_____

_____

_____

_____

_____

_____

_____

Now, do the same thing with your **emotions**. What are you feeling, right now in this moment? You may have a wide range of feelings mixed in with the anxiety. Set aside ideas about "right" or "wrong" feelings for a few minutes. Give yourself permission to feel whatever you are already feeling. You don't have to change them, fix them, analyze them, or make them go away. Again, just acknowledge them like old friends.

_____

_____

_____

_____

_____

_____

_____

Next, bring the same sense of curiosity to your thinking. What thoughts, images, or memories are moving through your mind right now? Again, explore them like a curious scientist. Just notice them as you would watch a movie, on a screen out in front of you. You don't have to fix, change, control, or stop any of the thoughts. Just acknowledge them, and list some below.

_____

_____

_____

_____

_____

_____

_____

Before ending this exercise, remind yourself that you are so much more than all of these experiences you are having. **Who you are is big enough that you can make room for all of these experiences.** They do not have to define you. It is okay to be you, even with anxiety.

Congratulations! You just bravely faced the anxiety monster! You may have found that it wasn't as scary as you thought. However, even if you feel worse now, you just taught yourself that you can face it! You don't have to always hide away. Instead of seeing your anxiety as impossibly overwhelming, you can just take it apart a little bit at a time.

Continue to practice this exercise in the coming weeks, and observe how your experiences change over time.

Resources

Recommended ACT Resources

WEBSITES

https://contextualscience.org
Association for Contextual Behavioral Sciences (ACBS)
This is the main website for the ACT community and all things ACT. Professionals have access to a listserv and to an online section of ACT-related handouts, videos, and other materials.

https://www.praxiscet.com
Praxis Continuing Education and Training
Provides information about in-person and online ACT training courses.

https://act.courses/signup
ACT courses developed by Steven C. Hayes, primary founder of ACT.

www.psych-insights.com
Author Richard Sears's website, containing resources, audio recordings, and videos.

RECOMMENDED READINGS

Bach, P., & Moran, D.J. (2008). *ACT in practice: Case conceptualization in acceptance and commitment therapy.* Oakland, CA: New Harbinger Publications.

Fleming, J. E., & Kocovski, N. L. (2013). *The mindfulness & acceptance workbook for social anxiety & shyness: Using acceptance and commitment therapy to free yourself from fear & reclaim your life.* Oakland, CA: New Harbinger Publications.

Follette, V. M., & Pistorello, J. (2008). *Finding life beyond trauma: Using acceptance and commitment therapy to heal from post-traumatic stress and trauma-related problems.* Oakland, CA: New Harbinger Publications.

Forsyth, J. P., & Eifert, G. H. (2016). *The mindfulness & acceptance workbook for anxiety: A guide to breaking free from anxiety, phobias & worry using acceptance & commitment therapy.* Oakland, CA: New Harbinger Publications.

Harris, R. (2019). *ACT made simple: An easy-to-read primer on acceptance and commitment therapy* (2nd ed.) Oakland, CA: New Harbinger Publications.

Hayes, S. C. (2020). *A liberated mind: How to pivot toward what matters.* Avery.

Hayes, S. C. (2007). *Acceptance and mindfulness at work: Applying acceptance and commitment therapy and relational frame theory to organizational behavior.* Binghamton, NY: Haworth.

Hayes, S. C., & Smith, S. (2005). *Get out of your mind and into your life.* Oakland, CA: New Harbinger Publications.

Hayes, S. C., Strosahl, K., & Wilson, K. G. (2012). *Acceptance and commitment therapy: The process and practice of mindful change* (2nd ed). New York: Guilford Press.

Luoma, J., Hayes, S. C., & Walser, R. D. (2017). *Learning ACT: An acceptance and commitment therapy skills-training manual for therapists.* Reno, NV: Context Press.

Ord, I. (2014). *ACT with faith: Acceptance and commitment therapy for Christian clients: A practitioner's guide.* Great Britain: Compass Publishing.

Sears, R. (2014). *Mindfulness: Living through challenges and enriching your life in this moment.* London, UK: Wiley-Blackwell.

Sears, R. (2017a). *The cognitive-behavioral therapy and mindfulness toolbox.* Eau Claire, WI: PESI Publishing & Media.

Sears, R. (2017b). *The sense of self: Perspectives from science and Zen Buddhism.* New York: Springer Nature.

Sears, R., Tirch, D., & Denton, R. (2011). *Mindfulness in clinical practice.* Sarasota, FL: Professional Resource Press.

Stoddard, J. A., & Afari, N. (2014). *The big book of ACT metaphors: A practitioner's guide to experiential exercises and metaphors in acceptance and commitment therapy.* Oakland, CA: New Harbinger Publications.

Tirch, D., Schoendorff, B., & Silberstein, L. R. (2014). *The ACT practitioner's guide to the science of compassion: Tools for fostering psychological flexibility.* New Harbinger Publications.

Walser, R., & Westrup, D. (2011). *Acceptance and commitment therapy for the treatment of post-traumatic stress disorder and trauma-related problems: A practitioner's guide to using mindfulness and acceptance strategies.* Oakland, CA: New Harbinger Publications.

Wilson, K. G., & DuFrene, T. (2009). *Mindfulness for two: An acceptance and commitment therapy approach to mindfulness in psychotherapy.* Oakland, CA: New Harbinger Publications.

References

Abrahms Spring, J. (2004). *How can I forgive you? The courage to forgive, the freedom not to.* New York: HarperCollins.

Alberini, C. M., & LeDoux, J. E. (2013). Memory reconsolidation. *Current Biology, 23*(17), R746–R750.

Association for Contextual Behavioral Science. (2020). *State of the ACT evidence.* Retrieved January 3, 2020, from https://contextualscience.org/state_of_the_act_evidence#

Avdagic, E., Morrissey, S. A., & Boschen, M. J. (2014). A randomised controlled trial of acceptance and commitment therapy and cognitive-behaviour therapy for generalised anxiety disorder. *Behaviour Change, 31*, 110–130.

Birnie, K., Speca, M., & Carlson, L. E. (2010). Exploring self-compassion and empathy in the context of mindfulness-based stress reduction (MBSR). *Stress and Health, 26*, 359–371.

Biron, M., & van Veldhoven, M. J. P. M. (2012). Emotional labor in service work: Psychological flexibility and emotion regulation. *Human Relations, 65*(10), 1259–1282.

Blackledge, J. T. (2007). Disrupting verbal processes: Cognitive defusion in acceptance and commitment therapy and other mindfulness-based psychotherapies. *The Psychological Record, 57*(4), 555–577.

Boeschen, L. E., Koss, M. P., Figuerdo, A. J., & Coan, J. A. (2001). Experiential avoidance and posttraumatic stress disorder: A cognitive meditational model of rape recovery. *Journal of Aggression, Maltreatment, & Trauma, 4*, 211–245.

Calhoun, L. G., & Tedeschi, R. G. (Eds.). (2014). *Handbook of posttraumatic growth: Research and practice.* New York: Routledge.

Covey, S. R. (1989). *The 7 habits of highly effective people.* New York: Simon & Schuster.

Craske, M. G., Niles, A. N., Burklund, L. J., Wolitzky-Taylor, K. B., Vilardaga, J. C. P., Arch, J. J., Saxbe, D. E., & Lieberman, M. D. (2014). Randomized controlled trial of cognitive behavioral therapy and acceptance and commitment therapy for social phobia: Outcomes and moderators. *Journal of Consulting and Clinical Psychology, 82*(6), 1034–1048.

Cromer, L. D., & Smyth, J. M. (2010). Making meaning of trauma: Trauma exposure doesn't tell the whole story. *Journal of Contemporary Psychotherapy, 40*(2), 65–72.

Foody, M., Barnes-Holmes, Y., & Barnes-Holmes, D. (2012). The role of self in acceptance and commitment therapy. In L. McHugh & I. Stewart (Eds.), *The self and perspective taking* (pp. 125–142). Reno, NV: Context Press.

Gloster, A. T., Klotsche, J., Chacker, S., Hummel, K., & Hoyer, J. (2011). Assessing psychological flexibility: What does it add above and beyond existing constructs? *Psychological Assessment, 23*, 970–982.

Gloster, A. T., Klotsche, J., Ciarrochi, J., Eifert, G., Sonntag, R., Wittchen, H., & Hoyer, J. (2017). Increasing valued behaviors precedes reduction in suffering: Findings from a randomized controlled trial using ACT. *Behaviour Research and Therapy, 91*, 64–71.

Harris, R. (2009). Mindfulness without meditation. *Healthcare Counselling and Psychotherapy Journal, 9*(4), 21–24.

Hayes, S. C. (2004). Acceptance and commitment therapy and the new behavior therapies: Mindfulness, acceptance, and relationship. In S. C. Hayes, V. M. Follete, & M. M. Linehan (Eds.), *Mindfulness and acceptance* (pp. 1–29). New York: Guilford Press.

Hayes, S. C. (2007). *ACT in action* [6-DVD series]. Oakland, CA: New Harbinger Publications.

Hayes, S. C. (2008). *Acceptance & commitment therapy (ACT): Helping your clients get out of their minds and into their lives* [Audio CD]. Eau Claire, WI: PESI.

Hayes, S. C. (2020). *Acceptance and commitment therapy.* Retrieved January 10, from https://contextualscience.org/act

Hayes, S. C., Luoma, J., Bond, F., Masuda, A., & Lillis, J. (2006). Acceptance and commitment therapy: Model, processes, and outcomes. *Behaviour Research and Therapy, 44,* 1–25.

Hayes, S. C., Strosahl, K. D., Bunting, K., Twohig, M., & Wilson, K. (2004). What is acceptance and commitment therapy? In S. Hayes & K. Strosahl (Eds.), *A practical guide to acceptance and commitment therapy* (pp. 3–29). New York: Springer.

Hayes, S. C., Strosahl, K., & Wilson, K. G. (2012). *Acceptance and commitment therapy: The process and practice of mindful change* (2nd ed). New York: Guilford Press.

Hollis-Walker, L., & Colosimo, K. (2011). Mindfulness, self-compassion, and happiness in nonmeditators: A theoretical and empirical examination. *Personality and Individual Differences, 50,* 222–227.

Kessler, R. C., Berglund, P., Delmer, O., Jin, R., Merikangas, K. R., & Walters, E. E. (2005). Lifetime prevalence and age-of-onset distributions of *DSM-IV* disorders in the National Comorbidity Survey Replication. *Archives of General Psychiatry, 62*(6), 593–602.

Kuyken, W., Watkins, E., Holden, E., White, K., Taylor, R. S., Byford, S., Evans, A., Radford, S., Teasdale, J. D., & Dalgeish, T. (2010). How does mindfulness-based cognitive therapy work? *Behaviour Research and Therapy, 48*(11), 1105–1112.

Lester, G. W. (2018). *Advanced diagnosis, treatment, and management of DSM-5 personality disorders.* Houston: Ashcroft Press; Eau Claire, WI: PESI.

Linehan, M. (1993). *Cognitive-behavioral treatment of borderline personality disorder.* New York: Guilford Press.

Linehan, M. (2014). *Skills training manual for treating borderline personality disorder* (2nd ed.). New York: Guilford Press.

Longmore, R., & Worrell, M. (2007). Do we need to challenge thoughts in cognitive behavior therapy? *Clinical Psychology Review, 27,* 173–187.

Luoma, J. B., & Vilardaga, J. P. (2013). Improving therapist psychological flexibility while training acceptance and commitment therapy: A pilot study. *Cognitive Behaviour Therapy, 42,* 1–8.

Mojtabaie, M., & Gholamhosseini, S. (2014). Effectiveness of acceptance and commitment therapy (ACT) to reduce the symptoms of anxiety in women with breast cancer. *Journal of Social Issues & Humanities, 4*(2), 522–527.

Moran, D. J. (2011). ACT for leadership: Using acceptance and commitment training to develop crisis-resilient change managers. *International Journal of Behavioral Consultation and Therapy, 7*(1), 66–75. http://dx.doi.org/10.1037/h0100928

Moran, D. J. (2013). Promoting psychological flexibility in clinical settings. *Behavior Analysis in Dentistry – Psicologia Odontoiatrica*, 21–27.

Nader, K., & Einarsson, E. Ö. (2010). Memory reconsolidation: An update. *Annals of the New York Academy of Sciences, 1191*(1), 27–41.

Neff, K. D. (2003). Self-compassion: An alternative conceptualization of a healthy attitude toward oneself. *Self and Identity, 2*, 85–101.

Neff, K., & Tirch, D. (2013). Self-compassion and ACT. In T. B. Kashdan & J. Ciarrochi (Eds.), *Mindfulness, acceptance, and positive psychology: The seven foundations of well-being* (p. 78–106). New Harbinger Publications, Inc.

Pennebaker, J. W. (1997). Writing about emotional experiences as a therapeutic process. *Psychological Science, 8*(3), 162–166.

Resick, P. A., Monson, C. M., & Chard, K. M. (2016). Cognitive processing therapy for PTSD: A comprehensive manual. New York: Guilford Press.

Sears, R. (2017a). *The cognitive-behavioral therapy and mindfulness toolbox.* Eau Claire, WI: PESI Publishing & Media.

Sears, R. (2017b). *The Ssnse of self: Perspectives from science and Zen Buddhism.* New York: Springer Nature.

Sears, R., & Chard, K. (2016). *Mindfulness-based cognitive therapy for PTSD.* London, UK: Wiley-Blackwell.

Sears, R., & Niblick, A. (Eds.). (2014). *Perspectives on spirituality and religion in psychotherapy.* Sarasota, FL: Professional Resource Press.

Segal, Z., Williams, M., & Teasdale, J. (2013). *Mindfulness-based cognitive therapy for depression* (2nd ed.). New York: Guilford Press.

Tauber, N. M., O'Toole, M. S., Dinkel, A., Galica, J., Humphris, G., Lebel, S., Maheu, C., Ozakinci, G., Prins, J., Sharpe, L., Smith, A., Thewes, B., Simard, S., & Zachariae, R. (2019). Effect of psychological intervention on fear of cancer recurrence: a systematic review and meta-analysis. *Journal of Clinical Oncology, 37*, 1–18. https://doi.org/10.1200/JCO.19.00572

Tirch, D., Schoendorff, B., & Silberstein, L. R. (2014). *The ACT practitioner's guide to the science of compassion: Tools for fostering psychological flexibility.* New Harbinger Publications.

Torneke, N., Barnes-Holmes, D., & Hayes, S. C. (2010). *Learning RFT: An introduction to relational frame theory and its clinical applications.* Oakland, CA: Context Press.

Ucros, G. (1989). Mood state-dependent memory: A meta-analysis. *Cognition & Emotion, 3*(2), 139–169. https://doi.org/10.1080/02699938908408077

van der Leeuw, J. J. (1928). *Conquest of illusion.* Adyar, Madras, India: Theosophical Publishing House.

Wampold, B. E., & Imel, Z. E. (2015). *The great psychotherapy debate: The evidence for what makes psychotherapy work* (2nd ed.). New York: Routledge.

Watts, A. (2004). *Learning the human game.* Louisville, CO: Sounds True.

Williams, M., Teasdale, J., Segal, Z., & Kabat-Zinn, J. (2007). *The mindful way through depression: Freeing yourself from chronic unhappiness.* New York: Guilford Press.

Wilson, K. G., & DuFrene, T. (2009). *Mindfulness for two: An acceptance and commitment therapy approach to mindfulness in psychotherapy.* Oakland, CA: New Harbinger.

Wilson, K. G., Sandoz, E. K., Kitchens, J., & Roberts, M. (2010). The Valued Living Questionnaire: Defining and measuring valued action within a behavioral framework. *The Psychological Record, 60,* 249–272.

Winnicott, D. W. (1964). *The child, the family, and the outside world.* England, UK: Penguin Books.

Yalom, I. D., & Leszcz, M. (2005). *The theory and practice of group psychotherapy.* New York: Basic Books.

Photo Credits

About the author. -Richard Sears. *Paul Wonji Lynch.*

1.1. Chinese finger trap.

1.3. Bucket with holes. *Ashlyn Karim.*

1.5. Lost in thoughts. *Jan Grafton.*

1.6. Inflexahex. *Stephen C. Hayes.*

1.7. Hexaflex. *Stephen C. Hayes.*

2.1. Waffleman. *Caylee Sears.*

4.1. Chessboard – Self as Content. *Richard Sears.*

4.2. Chessboard – Self as Context. *Richard Sears.*

4.3. Collage of Selves. *Richard Sears.*

5.1. Noticing thoughts without fighting them. *Jan Grafton.*

5.2. Train of thoughts. *Ashlyn Karim.*

5.3. Judgment factory. *Ashlyn Karim.*

6.5. Comforting younger self. *Jan Grafton.*

8.3. Tin can monster. *Ashlyn Karim.*

Made in the USA
Coppell, TX
02 July 2021